P9-AGU-732

On Speaking Terms 1

REAL LANGUAGE FOR REAL LIFE

ELIANA SANTANA-WILLIAMSON

HEINLE
CENGAGE Learning

Australia • Brazil • Japan • Korea • Mexico • Singapore • Spain • United Kingdom • United States

On Speaking Terms 1:

Real Language for Real Life

Eliana Santana Williamson

Publisher: Sherrise Roehr

Acquisitions Editor: Tom Jefferies

Assistant Editor: Marissa Petrarca

Director, US Marketing: Jim McDonough

Marketing Manager: Caitlin Driscoll

Content Project Manager: John Sarantakis

Print Buyer: Susan Spencer

Composition: Pre-Press PMG

Cover Designer: Muse Group, Inc.

Cover Image: Corbis

© 2010 Heinle, Cengage Learning

ALL RIGHTS RESERVED. No part of this work covered by the copyright herein may be reproduced, transmitted, stored, or used in any form or by any means graphic, electronic, or mechanical, including but not limited to photocopying, recording, scanning, digitizing, taping, Web distribution, information networks, or information storage and retrieval systems, except as permitted under Section 107 or 108 of the 1976 United States Copyright Act, without the prior written permission of the publisher.

For permission to use material from this text or product, submit all requests online at **cengage.com/permissions**. Further permissions questions can be emailed to **permissionrequest@cengage.com**.

Library of Congress Control Number: 2009935401

ISBN-13: 978-0-618-39600-9

ISBN-10: 0-618-39600-4

Heinle
20 Channel Center Street
Boston, MA 02210
USA

Cengage Learning is a leading provider of customized learning solutions with office locations around the globe, including Singapore, the United Kingdom, Australia, Mexico, Brazil, and Japan. Locate your local office at: **international.cengage.com/region**

Cengage Learning products are represented in Canada by Nelson Education, Ltd.

Visit Heinle online at **elt.heinle.com**
Visit our corporate website at **cengage.com**

Printed in the United States of America
1 2 3 4 5 6 7 8 9 10 — 13 12 11 10 09

Photo Credits

CHAPTER 1

Page 1: Left: © Adam Tinney/Shutterstock; Center: © Fjvsoares/Dreamstime.com; Right: © Ariel Skelley/Getty Images

CHAPTER 2

Page 19: © diego cervo/iStockPhoto

CHAPTER 3

Page 35: Top left: © Jetta Productions/Getty Images; Top right: © Grafissimo/iStockPhoto; Bottom: © Avava/Dreamstime.com Page 37: © Yellowj/Shutterstock Page 38: Left: © amygdala imagery/Shutterstock; Center: © Morguefile; Right: © Graca Victoria/Shutterstock

CHAPTER 4

Page 47: © Monkey Business Images/Shutterstock

CHAPTER 5

Page 67: Left: © Mark Stout/Dreamstime.com; Center: © Gamutstockimagespvtltd/Dreamstime.com; Right: © Redbaron/Dreamstime.com Page 71: © David Koscheck/Shutterstock Page 76: Top left: © Bornshtein/Shutterstock; Top center: © dyoma/Shutterstock; Top right: © Camuka510/Dreamstime.com; Bottom left: © Camuka510/Dreamstime.com; Bottom right: © Lepro/Shutterstock Page 77: Top left: © jocicalek/Shutterstock; Top right: © Ijansempoi/Dreamstime.com; Bottom left: © ifong/Shutterstock; Bottom right: © nyasha/Shutterstock

CHAPTER 6

Page 85: Left: © David Meharey/iStockPhoto; Right: © Svemir/Shutterstock

CHAPTER 7

Page 103: © Anna Bryukhanova/iStockPhoto
Page 117: © ColorBlinkd Images/Getty Images

CHAPTER 8

Page 123: Top left: © Dewayne Flowers/Shutterstock; Top right: © Smokefish/Dreamstime.com; Bottom: © Pali Rao/iStockPhoto

CHAPTER 9

Page 137: Left: © Ed Bock Stock/Dreamstime.com; Right: © Jason Stitt/Shutterstock

CHAPTER 10

Page 153: Top left: © Kiselev Andrey Valerevich/Shutterstock; Top right: © Khz/Dreamstime.com; Bottom: © Demid/Shutterstock

Contents

LISTENING STRATEGIES	PRONUNCIATION	GRAMMAR	CONTEXT
Meeting People			
• Listening for the main idea by building mental pictures	• Rising and falling intonation • Intonation used for asking and answering *yes/no* questions	• Simple present tense of *be* and action verbs	SOCIAL
• Listening for rising or falling intonation	• Intonation of *wh*-questions	• *Wh-* questions with *be* and action verbs • *Be* vs. action verbs	ACADEMIC
In Need of Words and Food			
• Listening for the main idea by building mental pictures (review)	• *It is* and *it isn't*	• Expressing doubt and possibility • Using modals to express doubt and possibility • *Yes/no* questions with *be* and action verbs (review)	SOCIAL
• Listening for details and taking notes	• Rising and falling intonation	• Complete sentence vs. sentence parts	SOCIAL
Explaining Problems			
• Listening for the main ideas and listening for details (review)	• Word stress with *can* and *can't*	• Explaining problems with *can* or *can't* • Using modals for suggestions • Sentence structure • Making Requests using *can* • Present progressive tense • Explaining problems with the present progressive tense • Expressing problems with the simple present, the present progressive, and *can't*	SOCIAL
• Listening for reductions: *wanna, gotta, hafta,* and *gonna*	• Reduced forms (reductions)	• Explaining problems • Expressing obligations, desire, and future plans • Making polite requests	ACADEMIC

To the Instructor

On Speaking Terms: Real Language for Real Life is a book that introduces the English Language Learner to *spoken language the way it is actually spoken,* that is, with its hesitations, pauses, grammar, and sounds present. Traditionally, listening and speaking textbooks have dialogs, or "spoken texts," that are scripted based on how the writers believe spoken language is constructed. *On Speaking Terms,* however, exposes learners to features of **real language,** such as, how to hesitate, how to ask for repetition, how to use grammar for speaking, how to connect thoughts as you speak, and many others.

FEATURES OF *ON SPEAKING TERMS*

REAL LIFE

On Speaking Terms is based on **real life** language. Researchers have recorded, transcribed, and analyzed real life interactions and have found that those real life interactions look very different from the spoken texts (dialogs) that appear in traditional speaking textbooks. Real life language does not "look" as "neat and perfect" as shown in most textbooks. For example, speakers don't always speak in complete sentences. When talking, we don't always say a sentence and then wait for the other speaker to say another sentence. That kind of "ping-pong" talk is not realistic. In real life, one speaker tends to dominate the conversation, whereas the listener acknowledges that he or she is listening with sounds and expressions, such as, *uh-huh, yeah, ok, right,* and so forth. In addition, speakers interrupt each other and talk at the same time. Speakers also react to what others say with expressions such as "you're kidding!" or "no way!" These are only a few of the features of real life language addressed in *On Speaking Terms.*

Chapters 1, 3, 4, 5, 6 and 9 present learners with language they can use within a social context, that is, in and around the community in which they live. They learn how to, for example, talk to friends and people they know, as well as speak politely and more formally with people they don't know. In Chapters 2, 6, 8 and 10, learners are also exposed to language within an academic context, that is, language that can be used in and around the school and workplace to communicate with their instructors, counselors, classmates, and managers.

REAL SPEAKING

Throughout *On Speaking Terms* learners are exposed to **real speaking** as they learn the grammar and features of speech. At the same time, they learn *how to be polite* as they use that grammar to communicate. In fact, some research studies show that pragmatics or appropriateness (politeness) mistakes are taken much more seriously by expert speakers of the language than grammatical mistakes are. Corpus linguistics studies also show that politeness is embedded in conversation. In fact, a researcher has stated that "conversation is expressive of politeness." Every chapter of *On Speaking Terms* contains Cultural Notes to help the English language learner understand how certain concepts are realized in American culture, and, how those concepts can be incorporated into speech.

REAL GRAMMAR

Another unique feature of *On Speaking Terms* is its **real grammar** presentation. Traditionally, textbooks that claim to teach speaking do not overtly teach grammar. Learners are put in groups, asked to discuss issues, and must attempt to construct spoken texts. In *On Speaking Terms,* however, learners study *the grammar of speaking*. Although many of the structures utilized in writing and in speaking are the same, grammar of spoken texts can be quite different from that of written texts.

In *On Speaking Terms,* you will notice that the structure of the language is presented in boxes. These boxes help learners visualize the arrangement of the linguistic components. Each part of speech (subject, verb, complement, etc.) is presented in a unique box. These boxes represent manipulatives (pieces that users can move around, or, manipulate). By having a mental picture of how grammar works, learners can manipulate the grammar for speaking and apply it to a vast number of situations, allowing them to be able to process grammar more quickly.

REAL LISTENING

Not only does *On Speaking Terms* introduce learners to real speech, but it also introduces students to **real listening.** Traditionally, listening is a skill that is tested only rather than taught. In most texts, learners listen to a conversation and answer comprehension questions. An outstanding feature of this textbook is *the teaching of listening*. Learners are introduced to concepts that promote real listening, such as making mental pictures as they listen to the main idea. If learners can figure out how to best process and remember main ideas, they will have a better chance to succeed when they are asked to answer question about these main ideas. Rather than just listening for key facts, learners are taught how to mentally process and remember what they listen to.

Many of the listening tasks in *On Speaking Terms* ask student to listen **before** they complete an exercise. These types of listening tasks provide learners with a sample of how people talk when doing a similar task. By listening to that model before they actually do the task, learners can participate in conversations with more confidence.

ORGANIZATION OF *ON SPEAKING TERMS*

CHAPTERS

On Speaking Terms has ten chapters. In Chapters 1, 3, 4, 5, 7, and 9, learners will be exposed to and learn how to engage in short social interactions and service encounters in the community where they live. Chapters 2, 6, 8, and 10 focus on the same skills from the preceding chapter, but students will use that language in the community where they study and work.

Each Chapter contains four distinct sections:

GET STARTED

Get Started introduces the learner to the context of the chapter by having learners look at a picture, listen to a conversation, and complete a simple task. Learners should then be able to start making connections between the new content of the chapter and what is already familiar to them. When learners can connect a new concept to what they already know, they can begin to identify information that is new to them.

LEARN AND PRACTICE

Learn and Practice is divided into four sections: Grammar, Speaking Strategies, Listening Strategies, and Pronunciation. It presents each new concept through scaffolding, and gives learners the opportunity to understand, process and practice the new concept in steps. Learners are presented with language (input) and are required to produce language as well (output). As they produce the language, the instructor has a chance to listen to the learners' language and give them feedback.

Grammar sections visually present the structure of the language. The elements that compose the structure of the language are presented in boxes which are moved around to show how the language works. The boxes are kept consistent throughout the book so learners can remember them. This should help any learner from any linguistic and cultural background remember how the English grammar of speaking works. Learners are asked to use grammar in different contexts (for example, at home or at school) and with different speakers (for example, with a friend or with an instructor) as well.

Speaking Strategies show learners strategies they can use to construct the language as they communicate. When we talk, we need to be able to listen to the speaker, understand the language, construct what we want to say, and say it. Oral communication can be quite complex, but there are strategies that can be used to lessen the burden and which will aid us in doing all these things in a matter of seconds. These strategies are taught throughout the book.

Listening Strategies introduce learners to strategies that can be used to help students listen and successfully process what they are hearing.

Pronunciation activities invite learners to notice how the mouth moves, rather than memorize phonetic symbols. By noticing how the mouth moves, learners should be able to process the information in a more efficient way. In addition, by learning to observe how the language is produced, learners become more independent and may be able to apply those strategies when out of the classroom.

REVIEW AND EXPAND

Learners will engage in simulations, role-plays, and games that provide them with a chance to expand the concepts learned to other contexts.

EVALUATION

Self-Evaluation aims to help learners develop their metacognitive skills. Therefore, learners will reflect upon their learning by checking how well they performed the particular skills taught in that chapter. It will invite the learner to think about what they need to work on and help them design an action plan for improvement.

SUPPLEMENTS FOR *ON SPEAKING TERMS*

AUDIO PROGRAM

◀◁)) The **Audio Program** was recorded in a way to provide learners with spoken samples that sound like real language. Learners will hear dysfluencies (reduced sounds, incomplete sentences, hesitations etc), simultaneous talk, interruptions, and so forth.

WEB MATERIALS

The web materials will contain instructor notes and assessment quizzes to accompany each chapter of the text. Instructor notes will explain the rationale behind the activities and provide simple and easy-to-understand explanations based on studies on language teaching and learning.

These materials will provide instructors with sound pedagogical explanations and help them develop as professionals.

By focusing on the real aspects of listening, speaking, and grammar, *On Speaking Terms* helps learners function in the community where they live, work, and learn.

Eliana Santana-Williamson

CHAPTER

1 | Who Are You?

GET STARTED

🔊 **ACTIVITY A**
CD 1 Track 1

Listen to three conversations. Write each conversation number below the corresponding picture.

a. _____2_____ b. _____1_____ c. _____3_____

ACTIVITY B Put the adjectives in the left column into one of the four boxes. Then add similar adjectives of your own.

American	**Physical Description**	**Personality**
athletic	athletic	friendly
tall	_____	_____
Brazilian	_____	_____
Chinese	_____	_____
dentist	_____	_____
friendly	**Nationality**	**Profession**
funny	American	dentist
nurse	_____	_____
responsible	_____	_____
small	_____	_____
student	_____	_____

 ACTIVITY **C**
CD 1 Track 2

1. Listen to the conversation. Two people are introducing themselves.

2. Work with a partner. Introduce yourself to your partner. Talk about your personality, your nationality, and your profession. Use the words from the box on page 1 and the useful expressions below to help you.

Useful Expressions

> Hi there, my name's Ana.

> Hello, I'm Carlos. I'm Mexican.

> Really? Me, too.

LEARN AND PRACTICE

SPEAKING STRATEGIES

Asking for Repetition and Spelling

Speaking and writing are different. In speaking, there is interaction between the speaker and the listener. If you don't understand what a speaker has said, you can ask the speaker to repeat things or spell out words. Here are some ways to:

Ask for repetition. ⟶	Excuse me? Could you say that again, please? What was that again?
Ask for spelling. ⟶	Can/Could you spell that, please? How do you spell that?

Checking Your Understanding and Confirming Information

You can check your understanding by repeating what you heard. The speaker can then confirm if the information is correct. Here are some ways to:

Check your understanding. ⟶	You said . . . ? Did you say . . . ? Was that . . . ?
Confirm information. ⟶	That's right/correct! Yes! Yep.

🔊 ACTIVITY **A**

CD 1 Track 3

Listen to the conversation. Two friends are looking at a photo album. Fill in the missing words.

A: So, who's this man?

B: Handsome, huh?

A: Yeah!

B: My grandpa.

A: No way!

B: Uh-huh.

A: Gee, he was good-looking!

B: I know!

A: What's his name?

B: Dimitri Pokrovsky.

A: _____excuse me?_____
(a)

B: Dimitri Pokrovsky.

A: _____How do you spell it_____
(b)

B: P-O-K-R-O-V-S-K-Y.

A: Russian?

B: Actually, that's interesting . . . he was Brazilian.

A: Really?

B: Yeah, but his dad, my great-grandfather, was Russian.

A: _____You said Russia?_____
(c)

B: _____
(d)

A: Oh, I see. He was *really* good-looking.

B: Yeah. My grandma says that all the time.

🔊 ACTIVITY **B**

CD 1 Track 4

1. Listen to the conversation. Two people are asking about personal information.

2. Work with a partner. Ask your partner for the personal information in the chart on page 4. Complete the chart with your partner's information. As you talk, ask for repetition and spelling, check your understanding, and confirm information.

Personal Information

Name: _____

Date of birth: _____

Place of birth: _____

First language: _____

Telephone number: _____

Three likes: _____

Three dislikes: _____

Simple Present Tense of *Be*: Statements with *You*

Be is the most common verb in English. *Be* is a strong verb. It doesn't need help or an auxiliary verb.

| You | are | strong. |

You and *are* can be contracted.

| You | 're | strong. |

You can be singular (refers to one person) or plural (refers to more than one person). In conversational English, *you guys* is sometimes used when addressing more than one person. Also, the contracted form *you're* is used frequently in conversational English.

ACTIVITY **C**   Imagine that you are talking to your best friend. Your friend has asked you to describe his or her personality. Write four sentences about your friend's personality. Use *you* and the verb *be*.

1. You are studious. _____

2. _____

3. _____

4. _____

5. _____

Simple Present Tense of *Be*: *Yes/No* Questions with *You*

To form *yes/no* questions with *be*, invert the subject and verb.

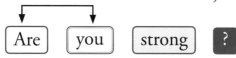

ACTIVITY **D** Write the sentences from Activity C as questions.

1. Are you studious? _____

2. _____

3. _____

4. _____

5. _____

Simple Present Tense of *Be*: Negative Statements with *You*

To make a negative statement, insert *not* after *be*.

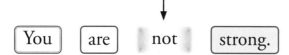

The contraction of *are not* is *aren't*.

In conversational English, the contracted forms *you aren't* and *you're not* are used much more frequently than the non-contracted form *you are not*.

ACTIVITY **E**   Write the sentences from Activity C as negative statements. Use the contraction *aren't* in two of the sentences.

1. <u>You are not studious. You aren't studious.</u>
2. _____
3. _____
4. _____
5. _____

Simple Present Tense of *Be*: Negative *Yes/No* Questions with *You*

We use negative *yes/no* questions to confirm information that we think we already know. For example, if I think I remember that José said he was 19 years old, I can ask, "Aren't you 19 years old?"

Use the contraction *aren't* in negative questions with *you*.

| Aren't | you | 19 years old | ? |

Affirmative Answers			Negative Answers		
Yes, I am.	Uh-huh.	Yep.	No, I'm not.	Uh-uh.	Nope.

ACTIVITY **F**   Write four negative questions with *you* and the verb *be*.

1. <u>Aren't you from Mexico?</u>
2. _____
3. _____
4. _____
5. _____

ACTIVITY **G**   Instructor Demo
1. In a small group, make a list of *Are you . . . ?* questions to ask your instructor.
2. Take turns asking your instructor your questions. Make sure you raise your hand before you start talking. Use the strategies in the box on page 7 when necessary. Find out as much as possible about your instructor.

Remember to...	• ask for repetition.	→	Excuse me?
			Could you say that again, please?
			What was that again?
	• ask for spelling.	→	Can/Could you spell that, please?
			How do you spell that?
	• check your understanding.	→	You said . . . ?
			Did you say . . . ?
			Was that . . . ?
	• confirm information.	→	That's right/correct!
			Yes!
			Yep.

Cultural Note   In American classrooms, it's important to make sure that everybody has a chance to speak during discussions. Raise your hand when you want to talk and wait for the instructor to call on you. Make sure you give others an opportunity to participate, too.

 ACTIVITY **H**
CD 1 Track 5

1. Listen to two students asking each other *Are you . . . ?* questions.

2. Work with a partner. Ask your partner *Are you . . . ?* questions. Refer to the Useful Expressions below to help your discussion.

3. Tell the class one thing you learned about your partner. Complete the sentence below.

I found out that _____ is _____ .
(partner's name)

Useful
Expressions

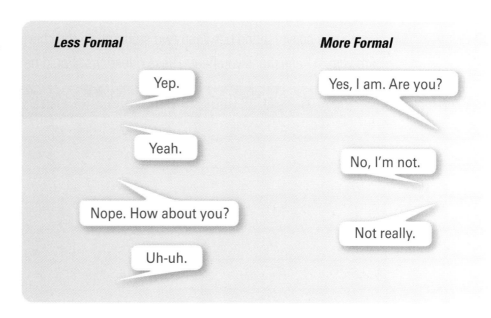

Less Formal

Yep.

Yeah.

Nope. How about you?

Uh-uh.

More Formal

Yes, I am. Are you?

No, I'm not.

Not really.

PRONUNCIATION

Rising Intonation

When we ask *yes/no* questions, we use <u>rising</u> intonation.

Listen and repeat.
CD 1 Track 6

Are you from Mexico?(↑)

Are you patient?(↑)

Are you a mother?(↑)

Are you a good student?(↑)

Falling Intonation

When we answer *yes/no* questions, we use <u>falling</u> intonation.

Listen and repeat.
CD 1 Track 7

Oh, yeah. I'm Mexican.(↓)

Not really.(↓)

Yes, I have two children.(↓)

Sometimes.(↓)

ACTIVITY 1
CD 1 Track 8

Listen to a conversation between two students. In the chart below, write down the *Are you . . . ?* questions you hear. These questions should have rising intonation.

***Are you . . . ?* Questions—Rising Intonation**

 ACTIVITY **J**
CD 1 Track 9

Listen to the conversation again. In the chart below, write down the responses to the *Are you . . . ?* questions you hear. These responses should have falling intonation.

Responses to *Are you . . . ?* Questions—Falling Intonation

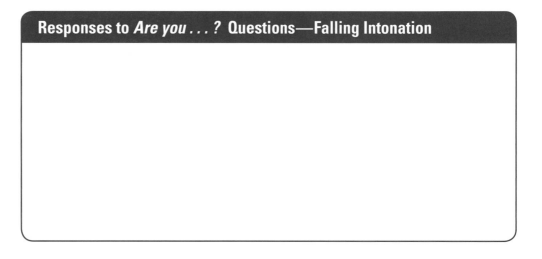 ACTIVITY **K**
CD 1 Track 10

1. Listen to a student trying to find classmates with the characteristics in the chart below.

2. Go around the room and ask your classmates if they have the characteristics in the chart below. Complete the chart with your classmates' names.

Remember to...		
• ask for repetition.	⟶	Excuse me? Could you say that again, please.
• ask for spelling.	⟶	Can/could you spell it, please?
• check your understanding.	⟶	You said...?
• confirm information.	⟶	That's right! Yes! That's correct.

Find someone who is . . .
organized. _____
very studious. _____
a vegetarian. _____
married. _____
single. _____
is a sports' fan. _____
from your country, too. _____

Listening for the Main Idea by Building Mental Pictures

As you listen for the main idea of what a person is saying, do not read, write, or do anything else. Focus on listening and try to imagine what is happening. Try to create pictures in your mind of the ideas you're hearing, as if you were creating a movie in your mind. This will help you to better understand the general ideas you hear.

🔊 ACTIVITY **L**
CD 1 Track 11

Listen to the conversation between two students. As you listen, build mental pictures of the ideas you hear. Answer the main idea questions below.

a. What are the woman and the man talking about? _____

b. Do they do the same things on the same days? _____

🔊 ACTIVITY **M**
CD 1 Track 12

1. Listen to the conversation again. In the chart below, write what the woman does during the week and what she does on the weekend. Write just the most important words and phrases—not complete sentences. Look at the example below.

Week	Weekend
gym 5X	

2. In pairs, compare your answers. Use the expressions below to help your conversation.

Useful
Expressions

> I heard that she goes to the gym three times a week.

> Oh, I heard something different. I heard five times, not three.

Simple Present Tense: Action Verbs

The simple present tense is the most common tense in conversational English. The simple present tense is often used with action verbs to express habits and routines.

ACTIVITY **N** Think about your week and weekend. In the chart below, write things that you usually do during the week and on weekends.

Week	Weekend
go to school	sleep in

Simple Present Tense of Action Verbs: Statements with I

| I | wake up | at 6:00 A.M. during the week. |

ACTIVITY **O**   Write sentences that describe things you do during a normal weekday. Use *I* and an *action verb* in each sentence.

1. I wake up early.
2. _____
3. _____
4. _____
5. _____

Simple Present Tense of Action Verbs: *Yes/No* Questions with *You*

To form *yes/no* questions with an action verb and *you*, insert *do* at the beginning of the sentence.

| Do | you | wake up | at 6:00 A.M. during the week | ? |

Affirmative Answers		Negative Answers	
Yes, I do.	Uh-huh.	No, I don't.	No, not really.
Yes, definitely.	Yep.	Definitely not.	Nope.

ACTIVITY **P**   Write the sentences in Activity O as *yes/no* questions with *you*.

1. Do you wake up early?
2. _____
3. _____
4. _____
5. _____

Simple Present Tense of Action Verbs: Negative Statements with I

Insert *don't* before the action verb to express a negative idea.

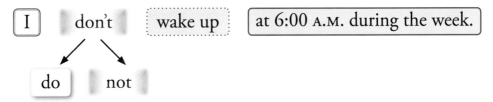

Don't use *not* by itself. *Not* almost always attaches itself to an auxiliary verb. In this case, it attaches itself to the auxiliary verb *do*.

ACTIVITY **Q**   Write the sentences in Activity O as negative statements.

1. *I don't wake up early.*_____

2. _____

3. _____

4. _____

5. _____

🔊 ACTIVITY **R**   Instructor Demo

CD 1 Track 13

1. Listen to a group of students asking their instructor *yes/no* questions about her activities during the week and weekend.

2. As a class, ask your instructor *yes/no* questions about his or her activities during the week and weekend. (Your instructor can only answer your questions using *yes* or *no*.) Your class can only ask a total of 20 questions. Find out as much as possible about your instructor's activities.

ACTIVITY **S**   As a class, choose one student to answer questions. Everyone else must ask that student *yes/no* questions about his or her activities during the week and weekend. Use the expressions on the next page to respond to the student's answers.

Useful *Expressions*

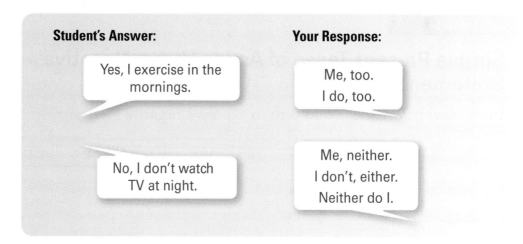

Student's Answer:

Yes, I exercise in the mornings.

No, I don't watch TV at night.

Your Response:

Me, too.
I do, too.

Me, neither.
I don't, either.
Neither do I.

GRAMMAR

Simple Present Tense of *Be*: *Yes/No* Questions in the Third Person

To form *yes/no* questions in the third person, invert *is* and the subject.

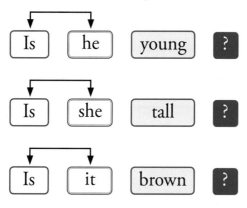

Affirmative Answers		Negative Answers	
Yes, it/she/he is.	Uh-huh.	No, it/she/he isn't.	No, not really.
Yes, definitely.	Yep.	Definitely not.	Nope.
		I don't think so.	Uh-uh.

ACTIVITY **T** One student in the class will think of a person, place, or thing. The rest of the class will ask *yes/no* questions with *be* to guess what the person, place, or thing is. Continue asking and answering questions until someone correctly guesses the person, place, or thing.

Simple Present Tense of Action Verbs: *Yes/No* Questions in the Third Person

To form simple present tense *yes/no* questions in the third person, use *does* + subject + verb.

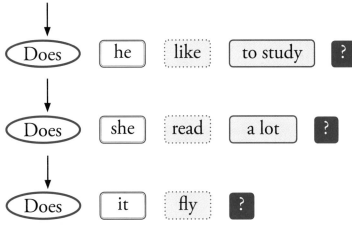

Affirmative Answers		Negative Answers	
Yes, he/she/it does.	For sure.	No, he/she/it doesn't.	Nope.
Yes, definitely.	Uh-huh.	No, not really.	I don't think so.
Yep.			

◀)) ACTIVITY Ⓤ
CD 1 Track 14

Instructor Demo

1. Listen to a group of students asking their instructor *yes/no* questions with action verbs. The students are trying to guess what animal their instructor is thinking of.

2. Your instructor will think of an animal. As a class, ask your instructor *yes/no* questions with action verbs to guess what the animal is. (Your instructor can only answer your questions using *yes* or *no*.) When you think you know the answer, raise your hand and ask, "Is it a . . . ?"

ACTIVITY **V**   One student in the class will think of an animal. The rest of the class will ask *yes/no* questions with action verbs to guess what animal it is. Continue asking and answering questions until someone correctly guesses the animal.

Simple Present Tense of *Be*: Statements with All Subject Pronouns

Study the statements with *be* and all of the subject pronouns.

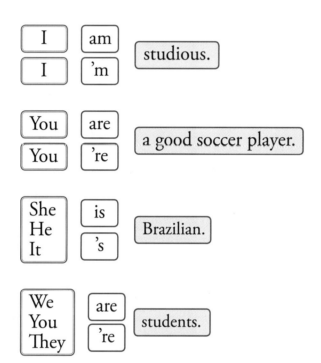

ACTIVITY **W**   Work in a groups of 5 or 6. Take turns making true statements about yourself and members of your group. Be sure to use all the subject pronouns.

REVIEW AND EXPAND

ACTIVITY **A**   Instructor Demo
Your instructor will imagine that he or she is a famous person. As a class, ask your instructor *yes/no* questions to guess which famous person he or she is thinking of. Use *be* and action verbs in your questions. When you think you know the answer, raise your hand and ask, "Are you . . . ?"

ACTIVITY **B**   Work in groups of three or four. Your instructor will give one student a famous person's name. Ask *yes/no* questions with *be* and action verbs. Try to guess which famous person the student is.

Remember to . . .	• ask for repetition.	→	Could you say that again, please? What was that again?
	• ask for spelling.	→	Can/Could you spell that, please? How do you spell that?
	• check your understanding.	→	You said . . . ? Did you say . . . ?
	• confirm information.	→	That's right/correct! Yep.

EVALUATION

ACTIVITY **A** Now that you have completed the activities in this chapter, complete the self-evaluation checklist below. Discuss your checklist with a classmate.

Self-Evaluation
Checklist

- [ ] I asked for repetition when I didn't understand.
- [ ] I asked my instructor to spell out the words that I didn't understand.
- [ ] I checked my understanding of the speaker.
- [ ] I confirmed information for the listener.
- [ ] I used the *be* verb and action verbs correctly.
- [ ] I used rising intonation with *yes/no* questions.
- [ ] I used falling intonation with answers.
- [ ] I built mental pictures when listening for the main idea.

ACTIVITY **B** Look back at the chapter and the self-evaluation checklist above. What can you do this week to improve the skills you have learned in this chapter? Talk with a partner and write an action plan for how you can improve your skills this week.

Example   I need to work on asking *yes/no* questions with action verbs. I will interview a family member using *yes/no* questions with action verbs. I'll focus on using the correct form of *do* in the questions. I will also focus on asking for repetition and checking my understanding when I talk to people.

Action Plan

2 | Can I Ask You a Few Questions?

GET STARTED

 ACTIVITY **A**
CD 1 Track 15

Listen to three conversations. In each conversation, a person is asking for a type of service. Complete the chart with the information you hear.

	Conversation 1	**Conversation 2**	**Conversation 3**
Where is the conversation taking place?			
What type of service is the person asking for?			

🔊 ACTIVITY **B**
CD 1 Track 16

Listen again. Write the *wh-* words (*who, what, when, where, why,* and *how*) used in each conversation. If no *wh-* words are used, write *none*.

Conversation 1: _____

Conversation 2: _____

Conversation 3: _____

ACTIVITY **C** **1.** Complete the chart below. What types of transactions can you do at each place? What information do you need for each transaction?

Place	Transaction	Information Needed
bank	*open a checking account*	*address*
library		
Department of Motor Vehicles (DMV)		
registrar's office		

CD 1 Track 17

2. Listen to a pair of students comparing their answers to the activity.

3. Compare your answers with a partner. Use the expressions below to help your conversation.

Useful Expressions

> At a library, you can check out books or return books.

> You need your library card.

LEARN AND PRACTICE

SPEAKING STRATEGIES

Asking for and Giving Personal Information in Transactions

When you complete a transaction, you often need to answer personal information questions. When you want to ask for information, use *wh-* questions.

What is your address?	**What is** your account number?
What's your address?	**What's** your account number?

ACTIVITY **A** Write four *What's your . . . ?* questions that you might need to answer during a transaction.

1. What's your _____

2. What's your _____

3. What's your _____

4. What's your _____

Asking Questions Politely

Questions that are asked during a transaction are usually more polite than during a casual conversation. Use *Can I / May I / Could I* + verb to ask a polite question.

Can I
May I   } **have** your telephone number?
Could I   **see** your ID?

Useful
Expressions

When we are asked a question, we should always respond in an appropriate way. Sometimes we use special expressions or sounds.

Sure. It's 223-4567.

Uh-huh. It's 270 Melrose Ave., Unit C.

Hold on. Let me get it.

 ACTIVITY **B**
CD 1 Track 18

Listen to the conversation. As you listen, try to build mental pictures to help you understand the main ideas. Then answer the questions below.

1. What information does the clerk ask for?

2. Where does the conversation take place? (More than one answer is possible.)

 ACTIVITY **C**
CD 1 Track 19

Listen again. Write the polite questions you hear on the lines below in the conversation.

1. **A:** Good morning. How can I help you?
2. **B:** Oh, yes. I need to change my address.
3. **A:** Sure. No problem.... _____
                                              (a)
4. **B:** Surazo.
5. **A:** _____
            (b)
6. **B:** Sure. It's S-U-R-A-Z-O.

7. **A:** _____
   (c)

8. **B:** Amalia.

9. **A:** OK, yes . . . I found it. Amalia Surazo.

10. **B:** Great.

11. **A:** And . . . _____?
    (d)

12. **B:** Sure. It's 1531 Middle Street, Apartment 202.

13. **A:** Uh-huh.

14. **B:** San Diego.

15. **A:** _____
    (e)

16. **B:** 92911.

17. **A:** Just to double-check. That's 1531 Middle Street, Apartment 202, San Diego, 92911.

18. **B:** Correct.

19. **A:** OK. _____
    (f)

20. **B:** Oh, um . . . it's the same. 218-555-5678.

21. **A:** All right! You're all set.

22. **B:** That's all?

23. **A:** Yes. Have a nice day.

24. **B:** Thanks. You, too.

SPEAKING STRATEGIES

Speaking Politely: Conversations with a Beginning, a Middle, and an End

Polite conversations generally have a clear beginning, a middle, and an end. Study the beginning, middle, and end of a conversation that takes place during a transaction.

Beginning: Opening Greeting/Introduction	Middle: Negotiating the Transaction	End: Final Comments / Closing
A: Good morning. How are you? **B:** Good. Yourself? **A:** Great. How may I help you?	**B:** I'd like/want/need to . . . **A:** Sure. Can I get your . . . ? **B:** Yes, it's . . .	**A:** All right. You're all set. **B:** Thanks a lot. **A:** Uh-huh.

ACTIVITY **D**   Go back to Activity C. Which lines of the conversation are the beginning, the middle, and the end of the conversation? On the lines below, write the line numbers for each part of the conversation.

1. Beginning: Opening Greeting _____

2. Middle: Negotiating the Transaction _____

3. End: Final Comments / Closing _____

 ACTIVITY **E**

CD 1 Track 20

1. Listen to two students role-playing a transaction.

2. Role-play transactions with a partner. One student will be Student A, and the other will be Student B. Follow the instructions below. Then switch roles and repeat the exercise.

Student A
• Imagine that you work in a bank, library, DMV, hospital, or another place where transactions occur. Write the place and three transactions that can be done at that place on a sheet of paper. Then display the paper on your desk.

• Write a list of polite questions using *Can I / May I / Could I + verb* that you will need to ask during each transaction. Then role-play a conversation with your partner.

Student B
• Pair up with a Student A. Read the place where Student A works and the three transactions. Choose a transaction that you want to complete. Then role-play a conversation with your partner.

Remember to . . .
• include a beginning, a middle, and an end in your conversation.

• use expressions such as *sure* and *uh-huh*.

• ask for repetition.   ⟶   Excuse me? Could you say that again, please?

• ask your classmates to spell it out.   ⟶   Can/could you spell it, please?

• check information.   ⟶   You said . . . ?

Wh- Questions with *Be* and Action Verbs

Wh- questions are very common in conversation. To form *wh-* questions, place the *wh-* word or phrase at the beginning of a *yes/no* question.

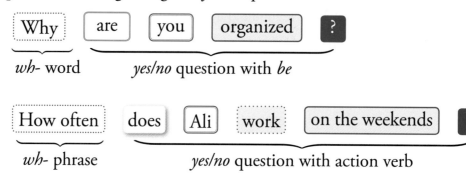

ACTIVITY **F** 1. Match each *wh-* word with the rest of the question. Write your answers on the lines. More than one answer is possible. How many different questions can you make?

1. What _____   a. do you go to school?

2. When _____   b. do you study on Saturdays?

3. How _____   c. do you have for math?

4. Who _____   d. is your favorite instructor?

5. Why _____   e. is your hardest class: math, biology, or Portuguese?

6. Where _____   f. is your chemistry class?

7. Which _____   g. is your first class?

CD 1 Track 21

2. Listen to a group of students comparing their answers to the activity.

3. In groups of three, compare your answers. Use the expressions below to help your conversation.

Useful Expressions

We can say, "What do you study on Saturdays?"

Yeah. Letters *b*, *e*, and *g* go with "What."

ACTIVITY **G**   Match each *wh-* phrase with the rest of the question. Write your answers on the lines. How many different questions can you make? More than one answer is possible. In groups of three, compare your answers.

1. How often _____   a. is this book?

2. What time _____   b. do you have English?

3. How much _____   c. do you live from school?

4. How many _____   d. is it to your apartment?

5. How far _____   e. TV sets do you have at home?

ACTIVITY **H**   Add a *wh-* word or phrase to the *yes/no* questions below.

1. _____ do you drink coffee?

2. _____ don't you like chocolate?

3. _____ is your favorite sport?

4. _____ is your birthday?

5. _____ is your favorite restaurant in town?

6. _____ do you like yellow?

7. _____ do you eat breakfast?

ACTIVITY **I**   Instructor Demo

1. Work in groups of three. Choose one person to be the secretary. Your instructor will tell the class an activity that he or she likes to do. Your group will have three minutes to think of *wh-* questions to ask your instructor about the activity. Come up with as many questions as you can. The secretary will write down the questions. The group with the most questions at the end of the three minutes wins.

Example   **Instructor:** I like exercising.

Students: Where do you exercise?   Why do you like to exercise?
                What kind of exercise do you do?   When do you exercise?
                How often do you exercise?   Who do you exercise with?
                What time do you exercise?

2. Ask your instructor your group's questions.

ACTIVITY **J**   Work in groups of four. One student tells the group an activity that he or she likes to do. The other three students take turns asking questions about that activity. The student answers the group's questions.

Intonation of *Wh-* Questions

In Chapter 1, you learned to use rising intonation with *yes/no* questions. However, when you ask *wh-* questions, use falling intonation.

🔊 **Listen and repeat.**

CD 1 Track 22

What's your name? (↓)

Where do you live? (↓)

🔊 **ACTIVITY K**

CD 1 Track 23

1. Listen to the questions. Which questions have falling intonation (↓)? Which questions have rising intonation (↑)? Check the correct answer.

	Rising Intonation	Falling Intonation
a. What's your first name?	☐	☐
b. What's your last name?	☐	☐
c. Are you single?	☐	☐
d. What time do you wake up?	☐	☐
e. Do you like sports?	☐	☐
f. Are you athletic?	☐	☐
g. What's your favorite sport to watch?	☐	☐
h. Do you like my questions?	☐	☐

2. Look at your answers above. Then write one sentence with rising intonation and one with falling intonation.

a. _____

b. _____

🔊 **ACTIVITY L** Listen to the questions again and repeat them using the correct intonation.

CD 1 Track 24

ACTIVITY **M** As a class, stand in two lines facing each other. Ask the student across from you one of the questions below. After the student answers, the student will ask you a different question. Monitor your partner's use of intonation. When you have finished, the students in one line take a step to the right (the student at the beginning of that line then moves to the end). Repeat the activity.

a. What's your first name?

b. What's your last name?

c. What's your favorite sport to watch?

d. What time do you wake up?

e. Do you like sports?

f. Are you athletic?

g. Are you single or married?

h. Do you like my questions?

SPEAKING STRATEGIES

Speaking versus Writing: Special Strategies for Conversations

There are some important differences between speaking and writing. When we write, we have time to plan, write, and revise our papers. When we speak, we have to think and talk at the same time. We often do not have time to think carefully about what we say or how we say it. As a result, speakers use strategies to help them gain time to think while talking, to change what they are saying, to clarify information when they don't understand, and so on.

Some of the strategies that speakers use include the following:

1. Hesitation (when a person's speech is interrupted by pauses or words such as *um*, or *uh*)

2. Repetition (when a person repeats a word: *I, I*)

3. Changing what he or she is saying mid-sentence (*Well, we can—I can go to the . . .*)

4. Using sentence parts (incomplete sentences)*

5. Using words or expressions that are not used in writing (*gosh, well, oh*)

*When you write, you must use complete sentences that have a subject and a verb. When you speak, you do not always need to use complete sentences.

ACTIVITY **N** 1. Read the two texts on page 28. Which one is a conversation? How do you know?

2. In the conversation on page 28, circle examples of the five special strategies presented in the box above.

Text 1	Text 2
A: Nice to meet you, Ms. Chen. I'm Anita Flores. **B:** Nice to meet you, Ms. Flores. **A:** Take a seat, please. **B:** Thanks. **A:** So, um, I see you're applying for the position of cashier. **B:** ...Right. **A:** Can you, I mean, how much experience do you have working as a cashier? **B:** I, um, I worked as a cashier for D-Mart for...for about eight years.... **A:** A long time! **B:** Yes, I liked it a lot. **A:** Why did you quit? **B:** Oh, I had a baby. **A:** Oh, I see. So, you're ready to come back to work? **B:** Uh-huh. **A:** OK, then, I, um, I'll give you a call tomorrow to let you know. I, I have two more people to interview. **B:** Thanks.	Dear Mom, I had a job interview today, and I think everything went pretty well. The interviewer asked me some questions about myself. I think I answered them with confidence. She seemed to be a very nice lady. She's the president of the company, but she seems very easygoing. She's going to let me know tomorrow. I need to go now. Call me whenever you have some free time. Love, Donna

🔊 ACTIVITY **0**

CD 1 Track 25

Listen and read along with the conversation below. Circle the things that are usually found in conversations but not in writing.

A: Hi. How are you?

B: Not bad. What can I do for you?

A: I need to, um...change my address.

B: OK. I need...to see your license.

A: Sure.... Here it is.

B: Now, um...what's the new address?

A: Uh, hold on, um...where's that paper?

B: You don't know your address?

A: It's my new...oh...wait. Here it is.

B: OK.

A: It's, uh, uh, 2471 Lark Avenue.

B: You said Park Avenue?

A: No—Lark.

B: Oh, thanks. The city?

A: Jamestown.

B: And the zip?

A: The zip, the zip's, um...oh, here. 29...45...7.

B: 29457?

A: That's correct.

B: OK. Sign here, please.

A: Where?

B: Here. On the line.

A: OK. Here it is.

B: Thanks. You're all set. Have a good day.

A: You, too.

The *Be* Verb versus Action Verbs

The *Be* verb and action verbs are different. The verb *be* doesn't need an auxiliary verb. Action verbs need the auxiliary *do* for questions and negatives in the simple present tense.

ACTIVITY [P] 1. Write the words below in the correct order. Add capital letters as needed.

> **Remember!** The *be* verb doesn't need help. To form a question, <u>invert</u> the subject and *be*. Add *not* after *be* for the negative.

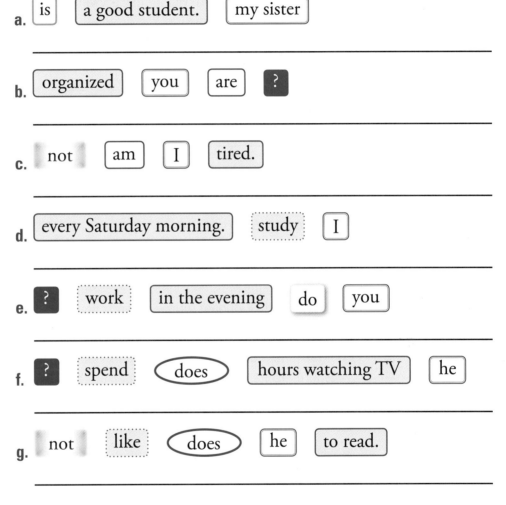

a. is | a good student. | my sister

_____

b. organized | you | are | ?

_____

c. not | am | I | tired.

_____

d. every Saturday morning. | study | I

_____

e. ? | work | in the evening | do | you

_____

f. ? | spend | does | hours watching TV | he

_____

g. not | like | does | he | to read.

_____

CD 1 Track 26

2. Listen to two students comparing their answers.

3. Compare your answers with a partner's. Refer to the expressions on page 30 to help your conversation.

Useful Expressions

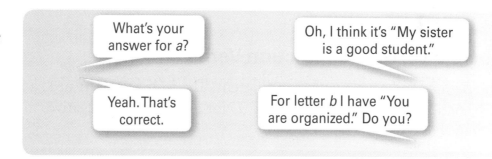

What's your answer for *a*?

Oh, I think it's "My sister is a good student."

Yeah. That's correct.

For letter *b* I have "You are organized." Do you?

ACTIVITY **Q** Answer the questions.

a. Action verbs need help. What auxiliary verb is used to help them?

_____

b. Look at sentences *f* and *g* in Activity P. Why is *does* used?

_____

c. When you want to ask questions with *be*, what do you invert?

_____

d. When you want to use the negative with *be*, what do you add?

_____

e. Where do you put *not*?

_____

ACTIVITY **R** **1.** Work in groups of three. One student writes different action verbs on index cards. Another student writes different forms of the *be* verb and the auxiliary verb *do*. The third student writes different subjects on index cards.

2. Trade index cards with another group. Use the subjects and verbs on the cards to form as many **statements** as you can. You may add your own objects to complete the sentences.

3. Then use the subjects and verbs to form as many **questions** as you can.

4. Make an index card with *not*. Form as many negative sentences and questions as you can.

Asking for Repetition and Spelling; Checking Your Understanding and Confirming Information

In Chapter 1, you learned how to

- ask for repetition. ⟶ Excuse me? Could you say that again, please?

- ask for spelling. ⟶ Can/could you spell that, please?

- check your understanding. ⟶ You said...?

- confirm information. ⟶ Right! / Yes! / That's correct. / OK.

◀)) ACTIVITY **S** Listen to the conversations. Which strategies are used in each conversation?
CD 1 Track 27 Check the boxes in the chart.

Speaking Strategy	Conversation 1	Conversation 2	Conversation 3
asking for repetition			
asking for spelling			
checking understanding			
confirming information			

Cultural Note   If you don't understand a word, a sentence, or any information that is important to the conversation, don't panic! Ask for repetition. Native speakers of English do this often.

REVIEW AND EXPAND

Speaking Politely: Conversations with a Beginning, a Middle, and an End

Polite conversations generally have a beginning, a middle, and an end. Like conversations that take place during a transaction, conversations during social interactions also have a beginning, a middle, and an end.

Beginning: Opening Greeting / Introduction	**Middle: Asking Questions**	**End: Final Comments / Closing**
A: Hi. How are you? **B**: Good. I'm Lina. **A**: I'm Vicki.	**B**: Where are you from? **A**: Brazil. What about you? **B**: Oh, I'm from Turkey.	**A**: It was great meeting you. **B**: Same here. Take care. **A**: You, too. Bye.

ACTIVITY **A** 1. Interview a partner about his or her likes and dislikes and schedule. Make sure your interaction has a beginning, a middle, and an end.

2. Then form groups of four and introduce your partner to the group. Remember to ask for repetition, ask for spelling, check understanding, and confirm information.

ACTIVITY **B** Role-play a skit in groups of three. Imagine that it is your first day of school. You want to meet new people. When you arrive at your classroom, there are two other students. Start a conversation with them. All three students should participate in the conversation. Do not forget to include a beginning, a middle, and an end in your conversation.

EVALUATION

ACTIVITY **A**   Now that you have completed the activities in this chapter, complete the self-evaluation checklist below. Discuss your checklist with a classmate.

Self-Evaluation Checklist

☐ I asked for personal information politely.

☐ I gave personal information when asked.

☐ My conversations had a beginning, a middle, and an end.

☐ I used the *be* verb and action verbs correctly in statements and *wh-* questions.

☐ I used special strategies, such as hesitation, in conversations when necessary.

☐ I used falling intonation with *wh-* questions.

☐ I asked for repetition and spelling when necessary.

☐ I checked my understanding and confirmed information when necessary.

ACTIVITY **B**   Look back at the chapter and the self-evaluation checklist above. What can you do this week to improve the skills you have learned in this chapter? Talk with a partner and write an action plan for how you can improve your skills this week.

Example   *I need to work on including a beginning and an end in my conversations. I'm going to study the beginning and ending parts of the conversations in this chapter again. I need to call my cell phone company this week. I'll practice those parts of a conversation when I talk to the customer service representative. I'll also practice it with two other people this week.*

Action Plan

CHAPTER

3 | What the Heck Is That?

GET STARTED

🔊 ACTIVITY **A**
CD 1 Track 28

Listen to three conversations. In each conversation, what word is the speaker trying to think of? Write the word below the appropriate picture.

a. _____

b. _____

c. _____

ACTIVITY **B**
Look around your classroom. Find an object that you don't know the name for. In groups of three, take turns describing the object while the other two students guess what it is. You can use a dictionary to help you.

LEARN AND PRACTICE

Expressing Doubt and Possibility

When someone asks, "What's that?" and we know the answer, we say, "It is a/an . . . " However, when we are not sure of the answer but think we might know, we often express possibility and doubt in our answer. Expressing doubt and possibility happens frequently in conversational English.

There are several ways to express possibility and doubt.

> **I think** it is a/an . . .
>
> It is a/an . . . , **I think**.
>
> OR
>
> It is **probably** a/an . . .
>
> **Perhaps** it is a/an . . .
>
> **Maybe** it is a/an . . .

Pronouncing *It Is* and *It Isn't*

When we say "It is . . . " and its negative form "It isn't . . . ," the individual words are pronounced together as one word. Look at the pronunciation below.

It is	= *itiz*	*It is* can be contracted to *It's*.
It isn't	= *idiznt*	*It isn't* can also be said as *It's not* or *It is not*.

CD 1 Track 29

Listen and repeat.

Maybe *it is* a watch.	Maybe *it's* a watch.
Perhaps *it isn't* a coin.	Perhaps *it's not* a coin.

 ACTIVITY **A**
CD 1 Track 30

Listen to the first part of each conversation. During the pauses, try to guess what objects the speaker is talking about. Use *it is* and *it isn't* when writing your guesses.

Conversation 1: _____

Conversation 2: _____

Conversation 3: _____

Conversation 4: _____

 ACTIVITY **B**
CD 1 Track 31

1. Listen to a group of students trying to guess the object in a "mystery photo."

2. Look at the mystery photo below. Work in small groups. Use *I think, probably, perhaps,* and *maybe* to guess what the object in the photo is.

3. Then check your answer on page 44.

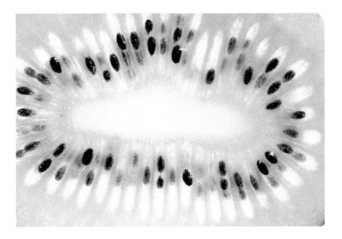

GRAMMAR

Using Modals to Express Doubt and Possibility

We can also use the **modal verbs** *could, might,* and *may* to express doubt and possibility.

> It <u>could be</u> a/an . . .
>
> It <u>might be</u> a/an . . .
>
> It <u>may be</u> a/an . . .

Could and *might* are the most common modals to express possibility in conversational English. *May* is also used, but it is not as common.

◀)) ACTIVITY C Listen to the conversation. Write the modals you hear in the conversation on the lines below.

CD 1 Track 32

> **A:** Stop the car! Look!
>
> **B:** What? Where?
>
> **A:** Over there. That blue balloon, or something . . .
>
> **B:** Gee. What the heck is that?
>
> **A:** I don't know . . . um, but it's not a plane.
>
> **B:** Um . . . well . . . it _____ be a plane.
> (a)
>
> **A:** No, it's not. It's not moving.
>
> **B:** You're right. It's not.
>
> **A:** What do you think it _____ be?
> (b)
>
> **B:** Um . . . it's a hot-air balloon. Or it _____ be a UFO!
> (c)
>
> **A:** Geez . . . UFOs don't exist!

◀)) ACTIVITY D 1. Listen to a group of students trying to guess the object in a "mystery photo."

CD 1 Track 33

2. Look at the mystery photos below. Work in small groups. Use *could, might,* and *may* to guess what the object in each photo is. If you know what the object is, say *it is.* Use the expressions below to help your conversation.

3. Then check your answers on page 44.

Useful *Expressions*

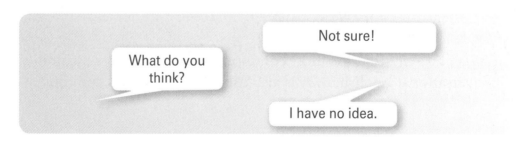

What do you think?

Not sure!

I have no idea.

ACTIVITY **E** Work with your group to make a "mystery drawing." Leave some white space at the bottom of the drawing. Put your group's drawing up on the wall of your classroom. Then try to guess the object in other groups' mystery drawings. Write your guesses in the white space below each drawing.

ACTIVITY **F** Work in a group of four. Then divide into two teams of two. Your instructor will give one student on each team the name of an object. The student draws a part of the object on a sheet a paper. The partner then guesses what the object is by asking *yes/no* questions: "Is that a . . . ?" The student who is drawing can answer, "No, it isn't," or "Yes, it is." If your teammate cannot guess the object, add more detail to the drawing. The first team to get the answer right wins. Remember to use rising intonation with *yes/no* questions.

Listening for the Main Idea by Building Mental Pictures

When you listen for the main idea, do not read or write as you listen. Focus on what you hear and try to imagine what is happening. Create a picture of what you hear in your mind. This will help you better understand the ideas you hear.

🔊 ACTIVITY **G** Listen to the two conversations. For each conversation, number the pictures in
CD 1 Track 34 the order they occur in the conversation.

CONVERSATION 1

a. _____ b. _____ c. _____

a. _____   b. _____   c. _____

Yes/No Questions with *Be* and Action Verbs

When forming *yes/no* questions with *be*, remember to put *be* in front of the subject. With action verbs, remember to add *do* before the subject.

Are	you	19 years old?	
Do	you	wake up	at 6:00 A.M. during the week?
Does	he	spend	too much time watching TV?

🔊 ACTIVITY **H**   Instructor Demo

CD 1 Track 35

1. Listen to a group of students asking their instructor *yes/no* questions. The students are trying to guess the place that their instructor is thinking of.

2. Your instructor will think of a place. As a class, ask your instructor *yes/no* questions to help you guess what the place is.

Example   Is it small?   Does it have a lot of doors?
                      Is it outdoors?   Does it have a swimming pool?

Use the speaking strategies below. Remember to raise your hand when you want to speak.

Remember to...		
• ask for repetition.	⟶	Excuse me? Could you say that again, please?
• ask for spelling.	⟶	Can/could you spell that, please?
• check your understanding.	⟶	You said . . . ?
• confirm information.	⟶	Right! / Yes! / That's correct.

ACTIVITY **1**   Work in groups of three or four. Your instructor will give you a card with the name of a place. Your group members will try to guess the place by asking you *yes/no* questions about the place.

SPEAKING STRATEGIES

Talking around a Word

Sometimes we forget a word or do not know the correct word to use when we are speaking. A speaking strategy that can help us communicate in those situations is *talking around a word*. People do this frequently in both their first and second languages. It is a very useful strategy. When you talk around a word, you explain the word without actually saying it. For example, if you have forgotten the word for *pencil,* you can use other words and phrases to describe it:

It's **made of** wood.
It's **used for** writing or drawing.
It's **in** schools and offices.
It **can be** long or short.
It **can have** different colors.

1. Listen to the conversation. A student is talking around a word, and her classmates are trying to guess what the word is.

2. Think of an object. Finish the description of the object in the squares below. As a class, take turns reading your description out loud to your classmates. They will guess what your object is. They can ask you more questions if necessary.

Object: _____

It's **made of** ⟶

It's **used for** ⟶

It's **in** ⟶

It **can be** ⟶

It **can have** ⟶

More Expressions for Talking around a Word

You can also use the expressions below to talk around a word.

What do you call that

| thingamajig
thing/thingy
stuff |

that

is	round?
can change	colors?
opens	cans?
makes	your hair shiny?

If you know what the word is, you can use the expressions below.

| I know what you mean. It's a/an . . .
You mean a/an . . . ?
Oh, I know. It's a/an . . . |

The word *stuff* does not have a plural *-s* form.

◀)) ACTIVITY **K**
CD 1 Track 37

Listen to three people describing some objects. First, listen and build a mental picture. During the pauses, write your guesses below. If you are sure of your answer, use these phrases: *I know. It's a/an . . . ; I know what you mean. It's . . . ;* and *You mean a/an . . .* If you are not sure, use **it could, it may,** or **it might be.**

Object 1: _____

Object 2: _____

Object 3: _____

Cultural Note   In American culture, it is acceptable to express doubt. In fact, if a person does not know or is not sure about information, the person should express doubt and possibility by simply stating, "I don't know," or "I'm not sure." It is inappropriate and considered dishonest to give wrong information.

ACTIVITY **L**   Work in groups of three or four. One student thinks of an object and talks around it. The other students try to guess what the object is. Repeat the activity until each student in the group has had a chance to talk around a word.

REVIEW AND EXPAND

ACTIVITY **A**   Your instructor will put objects in a bag or use a student's purse or backpack. Your instructor will describe each object by talking around a word. As a class, guess the objects in the bag. Remember to ask *yes/no* questions with rising intonation.

ACTIVITY **B**   Work in a group of three or four. One student will be the secretary. (The secretary is the only student who can write down ideas.) Your instructor will show you an object. Your group will have three minutes to think of things you can do with that object. The secretary will write down the group's suggestions. Refer to the expressions below to help your conversation.

Useful *Expressions*

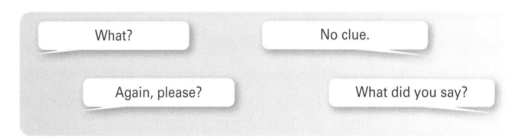

What?

No clue.

Again, please?

What did you say?

Remember to...	• ask for repetition.	→	Excuse me? Could you say that again, please?
	• ask for spelling.	→	Can/could you spell that, please?
	• check your understanding.	→	You said...?
	• confirm information.	→	Right! / Yes! / That's correct.

ANSWER KEY   Activity B, page 37:   inside of a kiwi fruit
Activity D, page 38:   a bicycle wheel
the skin of a pineapple
a zipper

ACTIVITY **C** 1. Work in groups of four. Use the cards on page 173 or make 10 cards with the name of an object on each card. Trade cards with another group.

2. Place the cards face down in a pile. The first student takes a card and talks around the object by describing the object as if he or she didn't know the name of it. The other three students guess what the object is. The first student to guess correctly keeps the card. The goal of the game is to collect as many cards as possible.

Remember to...
- talk around the word.   ⟶   What do you call that thing that...?
- respond.   ⟶   You mean...?
- talk about possible uses.   ⟶   It can be used to...

EVALUATION

ACTIVITY **A** Now that you have completed the activities in this chapter, complete the self-evaluation checklist below. Discuss your checklist with a classmate.

Self-Evaluation Checklist

- ☐ I used modals to express doubt and possibility.
- ☐ I correctly pronounced *it is* and *it isn't*.
- ☐ I listened for the main idea by building mental pictures.
- ☐ I talked around words when necessary.
- ☐ I asked questions with *be* correctly.
- ☐ I asked questions with action verbs correctly.

ACTIVITY **B** Look back at the chapter and the self-evaluation checklist above. What can you do this week to improve the skills you have learned in this chapter? Talk with a partner. Turn to the next page and write an action plan for how you can improve your skills this week.

Example   *I need to work on expressing possibility. I'm going to study that part of the chapter more closely. I will come up with sentences that express possibility and practice them aloud. I'll see a tutor to practice the sentences or ask a friend to chat with me. While talking, I'm going to focus on using modals that express possibility.*

Action Plan

GET STARTED

 ACTIVITY **A**
CD 2 Track 1

Listen to three conversations. Each conversation takes place at an international restaurant. Circle the type of restaurant that each conversation takes place in.

Conversation 1:   **a.** Balinese   **b.** Brazilian   **c.** Argentinean

Conversation 2:   **a.** Lebanese   **b.** Mexican   **c.** Brazilian

Conversation 3:   **a.** Malaysian   **b.** Italian   **c.** French

 ACTIVITY **B**
CD 2 Track 2

1. Listen to a group of students discussing the kinds of ethnic food they like.

2. In a small group, talk about the kinds of ethnic food you like. Find out if your group likes the same kinds of ethnic food you do.

ACTIVITY **C** 1. In the United States, there are many kinds of restaurants. Complete the chart below. For each type of restaurant, write if it is informal or formal, give examples of specific restaurants you know, and list some of the foods you can eat there.

Type of Restaurant	Informal or Formal?	Examples	Foods You Can Eat There
hotel restaurant			
fast-food restaurant			
ice cream shop			
small family-owned restaurant			
pizzeria			
submarine sandwich shop*			

*Note: Submarine sandwiches may have a different name in different areas. They are also called *subs, hoagies, or grinders.* Ask your instructor.

CD 2 Track 3

2. Listen to a pair of students comparing their answers.

3. Compare your answers with a partner. Use the expressions below to help your conversation.

Useful Expressions

What do you have for "hotels"?

I think hotel restaurants are formal. What about you?

Um, I think we can eat pasta there, seafood, stuff like that.

ACTIVITY **D** Organize the foods in the box below by type: appetizers (sometimes called *starters*), entrées (sometimes called *main courses*), side dishes (sometimes called *sides*), drinks (sometimes called *beverages*), and desserts. Write the words in the appropriate boxes.

salad	buffalo wings	chips with salsa
cake	soup	shrimp with vegetables
iced tea	ice cream	veggie burger
french fries	rice	spaghetti with meatballs
coleslaw	mashed potatoes	smoothie
water	corn on the cob	fried chicken
grilled salmon	soda	mozzarella sticks

Appetizers	Entrées	Side Dishes	Drinks	Desserts

LEARN AND PRACTICE

Listening for Details

In Chapters 1 and 3, you learned how to listen for the main idea. In this chapter, you will learn how to listen for details. Details are specific pieces of information—things you need to write down or you will forget. Some examples of details are telephone numbers, addresses, names, and dates. As you hear details, take quick notes to help you remember the information better.

The steps in the chart below show you what to do before, during, and after a listening task to help you improve your ability to listen for details.

Before the Listening Task	During the Listening Task	After the Listening Task
• Read the questions. Find out what information you need to listen for. • Be ready to take brief notes on what you hear.	When you hear the information, do not write everything. Take notes and write just enough to help you remember it. Use abbreviations, such as *rest.* for *restaurant.*	Read your notes. Then answer the questions.

Look at how one student took notes and wrote final answers to a listening task.

Questions	Notes Taken during the Listening Task	Final Answers to Questions
number of people?	3	three
drinks ordered?	soda / cof. / H$_2$O	soda, coffee, and water
appetizers ordered?	buf. wings	buffalo wings
entrées ordered?	fish + mash pot. veg burg chz piz	fish with mashed potatoes, a veggie burger, and a cheese pizza
desserts ordered?	0	none
total bill?	35	$35.00

ACTIVITY **A** For the listening tasks below, follow the steps for before, during, and after a listening task from page 50.

    1. a. Read the questions below to find out the details you need listen for.

CD 2 Track 4

    b. Listen to a conversation at a restaurant. Take notes on the details you hear.

    c. After you listen to the conversation, use your notes to complete the chart below. Then listen to the conversation again and check your answers.

Conversation 1	Notes	Answers
Name of the restaurant?		
Number of people?		
Drinks ordered?		
Appetizers ordered?		
Entrées ordered?		
How steak was cooked?		
Side dishes ordered?		

    2. a. Read the questions below to find out the details you need to listen for.

CD 2 Track 5

    b. Listen to a conversation at a restaurant. Take notes on the details you hear.

    c. After you listen to the conversation, use your notes to complete the chart below. Then listen to the conversation again and check your answers.

Conversation 2	Notes	Answers
Name of the restaurant?		
Number of people?		
Sandwich ordered?		
Type of dressing ordered?		
For here or to go?		
Dessert ordered?		
Total bill?		

Ordering in Restaurants

It's very simple to order in restaurants. Look at the expressions below.

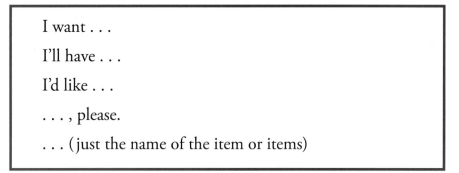

> I want . . .
>
> I'll have . . .
>
> I'd like . . .
>
> . . . , please.
>
> . . . (just the name of the item or items)

Cultural Note In sit-down restaurants, the host or hostess will usually ask for the number of people in your group before they seat you. In this situation, the word *party* is often used to mean group: *How many people in your party?*

🔊 **ACTIVITY B**
CD 2 Track 6

Listen to the conversation and answer the questions. Discuss the answers with the class.

    a. Are they at a fast-food restaurant? How do you know?

    b. Are they vegetarian?

    c. Do they order appetizers?

🔊 **ACTIVITY C**
CD 2 Track 7

Listen again. Now answer the questions about details. Get ready to write the answers down as you hear them.

    a. What do they order to drink and eat? _____

    _____

    b. How does the man want the steak cooked? _____

    _____

1. Listen again and write the expressions they use to order in the conversation.

Hostess: Welcome to Green Garden. A party of two?

Woman: Yes.

Hostess: Please follow me. . . Your server will be with you in a minute.

Woman: Thanks.

Waiter: How are you doing tonight?

Woman: Great! Yourself?

Waiter: Pretty good. My name is Roberto, and I'm going to be your server tonight. Can I get you something to start with—a drink?

Woman: _____, please.
                    (a)

Man: I _____ beer.
              (b)

Waiter: Any appetizers?

Woman and Man: No, thanks.

Waiter: Do you need some time to take a look at the menu?

Woman: Actually, we're ready.

Waiter: All right. What can I get for you?

Woman: _____ the grilled salmon with vegetables.
                    (c)

Waiter: Uh-huh. A soup or salad for a dollar more?

Woman: No, thanks.

Waiter: You, sir?

Man: _____
                (d)

Waiter: How do you want your steak cooked?

Man: Medium rare.

Waiter: Soup or salad?

Man: _____
                (e)

Waiter: Italian, ranch, or honey mustard?

Man: _____
                (f)

Waiter: Anything else?

Man: That's all.

Waiter: I'll be right back with your drinks.

2. Imagine your instructor is a waiter. Raise your hand and order something to drink or eat from your instructor.

Taking Orders in Restaurants

It is also very simple to take orders. Read the examples below.

What	would you like to eat/drink?
	can I get (for) you?
	do you want/need?

| How | do you want your steak cooked? |

Anything to drink?

Any dessert?

Water?

Soup or salad?

Do you need/want . . . ?

ACTIVITY **E** **1.** Write expressions used for taking orders on the lines below in the conversation. More than one answer is possible.

A: Good evening. My name is Earl. _____ something to drink?

(a)

B: Sure. Water for me.

C: A soda, please.

A: OK. _____ appetizer?

(b)

B: I'm fine. Do you want an appetizer?

C: No, I'm OK.

B: No, thanks.

A: _____ a few more minutes?

(c)

B and C: Yes, please.

A: I'll be right back with your drinks.

Five minutes later . . .

A: All right. Are you ready?

B: Yes. Um, I want a, um . . . the fish tacos . . . the ones right here.

A: OK. And you, sir?

C: The sirloin steak, please.

A: _____ it cooked?
   (d)

C: Medium rare.

A: OK. Soup _____ salad?
   (e)

C: Salad.

A: Ranch, Italian, or honey mustard?

C: Ranch.

A: Is that all?

B and C: Yes.

2. Role-play a restaurant scene with a partner. One person is the server (waiter/waitress), and the other is the customer. Look at the menu on page 60. The server asks questions, and the customer orders the food.

GRAMMAR

Complete Sentence (Formal) versus Sentence Parts (Informal)

In speaking, both formal and informal language is used, depending on the situation. In formal language, complete sentences are often used. The more informal the language, the more sentence parts are used. Sentence parts are phrases that are not complete sentences.

Complete Sentences (Formal)	Sentence Parts (Informal)
I'd like to have a turkey sandwich on whole wheat with Swiss.	A turkey sandwich on whole wheat with Swiss.
Would you like anything to drink?	Anything to drink?
I'll have some water.	Just water.

Cultural Note   In American culture, you should *not* snap your fingers or make noises to call the server to your table. This is considered impolite. Make eye contact with the server and ask him or her to come over by saying, "Excuse me."

1. Read the conversations below. Circle examples of sentence parts and underline complete sentences.

Conversation 1	Conversation 2
A: Good evening, Dr. Alvarez.	**A:** Welcome to Subshop! Are you both ready?
B: How are you?	**B:** I wanna . . . um . . . roasted chicken sandwich on wheat . . .
A: What can I get you to drink?	
B: May I have the wine list?	**A:** A nine-inch?
A: Certainly, sir. Ma'am?	**B:** Six, please.
C: I'd like to have some black tea.	**A:** Cheese?
A: Certainly. Let me know when you are ready.	**B:** Swiss.
	A: Lettuce, tomato?
B: Waiter.	**B:** Oh, yes, I want lettuce, onions, olives, and tomatoes.
A: Yes, sir?	
B: I'll have the house wine tonight.	**A:** Uh-uh. Dressing?
A: Great choice, sir.	**B:** Oh, and honey mustard.
B: Now, I, uh . . . I'll have the lobster special.	**A:** For here or to go?
A: Yes, sir.	**B:** To go, please.
C: And I'd like the shrimp alfredo.	**A:** Do you want the combo?
A: Would you like an appetizer to start with?	**B:** No, thanks. How much is the cookie?
B: No, thank you. That's all.	**A:** 60 cents.
A: I'll be right back with your drinks.	**B:** Can I get two?
	A: Sure. 6.50.
	B: I'm paying for my friend's, too.
	A: Oh, just chips . . . 99 cents more . . . 7.49.
	B: Here you go.
	A: Out of ten? Here's your change. Thanks. Have a good day.
	B: Thanks. You, too.

2. Both conversations have complete sentences and sentence parts. However, one conversation has more sentence parts, which shows that it is more informal than the other conversation. Which conversation is more informal? _____

Following a Script in Restaurants

Just like in a play where actors use a script, when we want service in a restaurant or dining establishment, there is usually an expected dialog, or "script," to follow, depending on where the service takes place. There is also vocabulary specific to each situation.

Read this "script" below:

A: Good evening, My name is Steve, and I'm going to be your server tonight. Would you like to start with something to drink? Maybe an appetizer?

Look at the language that is used in the script. You know that, based on what is being said (the script), this is not a cafeteria or a fast-food restaurant. The speaker is using more formal language and is speaking in complete sentences. You also see the vocabulary used, such as *server* and *appetizer*, and you know these words are probably not used at a fast-food restaurant, deli, or cafeteria.

So, based on the script, it is likely that this is a regular sit-and-dine restaurant. By paying attention to the language and vocabulary of a script, you can usually determine where the speakers are, and if they are in a more or less formal situation.

ACTIVITY **G** Read the conversation "scripts" below. Discuss with a partner the type of restaurant each conversation takes place at. How do you know?

Conversation 1	Conversation 2	Conversation 3
A: Good evening. A table for three? **B:** Yes, please. **A:** Name? **B:** Todd. **A:** With two *d*s? **B:** Uh-huh. **A:** It'll be about 30 minutes. **B:** OK.	**A:** Hi. How are you? **B:** Good. Yourself? **A:** Great. **B:** The line's long today, huh? **A:** It's always like this between 12:00 and 1:00. Students are out of class. **B:** Yeah. OK, um . . . today I want . . . the spaghetti with meatballs. **A:** Here you are. You can get a soda for free with your meal. **B:** Great! Thanks!	**A:** Next. Hello. **B:** Hi. Um . . . I want, um . . . turkey . . . on wheat. **A:** Cheese? **B:** Swiss, please. **A:** Anything else? **B:** No, thanks. **A:** Mustard or mayo? **B:** A little bit of both. **A:** Lettuce, tomatoes? **B:** Everything. **A:** Your total is $5.50. Out of 20? Here's your change. **B:** Thank you.

Cultural Note
Different cultures have different customs for different services. For example, in certain cultures, the tip is included in the bill. In American culture, though, the tip is usually not included in the bill. You need to tip a server between 15% and 20% if the service is good. The tip only comes included if you are dining with a big group.

REVIEW: LISTENING FOR THE MAIN IDEA BY BUILDING MENTAL PICTURES

 ACTIVITY **H**
CD 2 Track 9

1. Listen to the conversations. Discuss with a partner what is culturally inappropriate in each situation.

> In this listening task, listen for the main idea, not details. You do not need to write anything. Just listen and try to imagine what is happening.

2. In groups, discuss one or two cultural differences between restaurant culture in your country and in the United States.

Cultural Note
When you eat at a formal restaurant, it is expected that you use formal language. This is considered polite. Informal language is acceptable at informal restaurants. Just like the type of clothes you wear, your language should match how formal or informal the restaurant is.

ACTIVITY **I**
CD 2 Track 10

Listen to the conversations. For each conversation, circle the type of restaurant that the people are in. Remember: You are going to listen for the main idea, not details.

Conversation 1:   **a.** pizzeria   **b.** local family-owned restaurant   **c.** cafeteria

Conversation 2:   **a.** sandwich shop   **b.** local family-owned restaurant   **c.** hotel restaurant

Conversation 3:   **a.** local family-owned restaurant   **b.** sandwich shop   **c.** cafeteria

 ACTIVITY **J**

CD 2 Track 11

Listen to the three conversations again. In the boxes below, write examples of formal and informal language you hear.

Conversation 1	Conversation 2	Conversation 3

ACTIVITY **K**

1. Work in a group of three. Your instructor will give you a card with the name of a restaurant on it and whether it is formal or informal. Create a short skit that takes place at the restaurant. One person plays the server, and the other two play the customers. Remember to use formal or informal language to match your restaurant.

2. Perform your skit for your classmates. Have them guess what kind of restaurant it is.

REVIEW: SPEAKING STRATEGIES

Talking around a Word

Sometimes you may not know the name of an item you want to order at a restaurant. You can use the speaking strategy *talking around a word* that you learned in Chapter 3 to help you when you order.

1. Listen to a pair of students role-playing a restaurant scene.

2. You are going to work in small groups. Choose an item from the menu below. Take turns role-playing a customer who wants to order this item but does not know the word for it. Use the *talking around a word* strategy and the expressions below to help you. Your group guesses the item you want to order.

Menu	
Appetizers	**Side Dishes**
Buffalo Wings	Vegetable Medley
Chips with Salsa	French Fries
Potato Skins	Baked Potato
Mozzarella Sticks	Onion Rings
	Caesar Salad
Entrées	**Drinks**
Chicken Caesar Salad	Soda
Steak Tips	Lemonade
Fried Fish Sandwich	Juice
Bacon Cheeseburger	Coffee or Tea
Shrimp with Pasta	**Desserts**
Fish and Chips	Ice Cream
	Brownie
	Apple Pie

Useful Expressions

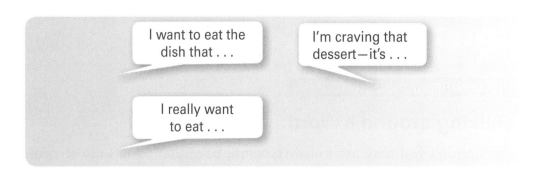

I want to eat the dish that . . .

I'm craving that dessert—it's . . .

I really want to eat . . .

Rising and Falling Intonation

In Chapter 1, you learned that when you ask *yes/no* questions, you use <u>rising</u> intonation. You also learned that when you answer *yes/no* questions, you use <u>falling</u> intonation.

🔊 Listen and repeat.

CD 2 Track 13

> Are you an artist?(↑)

> Yes. And a good one.(↓)

In Chapter 2, you learned that we use <u>falling</u> intonation with *wh-* questions.

> What's your name?(↓)

> Where do you live?(↓)

🔊 ACTIVITY **M**

CD 2 Track 14

Listen to the conversation between a waitress and a customer. Draw an arrow pointing up (↑) for rising intonation and an arrow pointing down (↓) for falling intonation.

Waitress: Hi. I'm Sue, and I'm your waitress today.
Do you want to order drinks? _____

Man: I'll just have water. _____

Woman: What else do you have to drink? _____

Waitress: We have soda, lemonade, and iced tea.
What would you like? _____

Woman: Lemonade, please. _____

Waitress: Are you ready to order now? _____

Man: Can we have a few minutes? _____

Waitress: Sure. _____

Later . . .

Waitress: Hi. Are you ready now? _____

Man: Yes. I'll have a burger. _____

Woman: And I want a veggie burger. _____

Waitress: What do you want on your burgers? _____

Man: Can you put the lettuce, tomato, and onion on the side? _____

Woman: Same for me. _____

Waitress: Sure. Anything else? _____

Man: Some onion rings, please. _____

Waitress: No problem. _____

 ACTIVITY **N**
CD 2 Track 15

1. Listen to the sentences without words. Use the intonation to decide if the sentence is a *yes/no* question or an answer to a *yes/no* question. Circle the correct answer.

    a. *yes/no* question   answer

    b. *yes/no* question   answer

    c. *yes/no* question   answer

    d. *yes/no* question   answer

CD 2 Track 16

2. Listen to the sentences again, this time with words. Were your answers correct?

ACTIVITY **O**

In pairs, pronounce the sentences below. Your partner has to say, "That's correct," or correct your intonation if it's incorrect.

    What time is it?   Are you from Argentina?

    Is it ten o'clock?   How do you like your food?

    Where are you from?   Do you like your juice?

    Who is this person?

REVIEW AND EXPAND

ACTIVITY **A**

As a class, role-play a scene at a formal restaurant. One student plays the restaurant host or hostess. This person greets and seats each party. The rest of the class divides into groups of three—two people act as customers and the third person acts as their server. After the host or hostess has seated everyone, he or she can join the last party as a customer or as the server.

Use the steps for what happens at a restaurant below as a guide for your role-play.

Step 1: When customers enter a restaurant, they look for the host or hostess.

Step 2: The host or hostess asks the customers, "How many people in your party?"

Step 3: The host or hostess takes the customers to their table.

Step 4: The customers wait for their server to come to their table.

Step 5: The server greets the customers. The server introduces himself or herself.

Step 6: The server asks the customers if they want drinks or appetizers. The customers respond.

Step 7: The server takes their orders. The customers respond. (Use the menu on page 174.)

Step 8: The server asks if the food is OK and if the customers need anything. The customers respond.

Step 9: The server asks if the customers are ready for the check. The customers respond.

ACTIVITY **B** With a partner, role-play a scene at a cafeteria. One student plays a cafeteria worker (W), and the other plays a customer (C). Use the menu on page 64. Use the conversation below as a model. Remember to use rising intonation with *yes/no* questions and falling intonation with *wh-* questions and answers to *yes/no* questions.

Placing an Order at a Cafeteria

Beginning:	**Middle:**	**End:**
C: How are you doing?	**W:** What can I get you today?	**W:** Have a good day.
W: Good. And yourself?	**C:** A chicken enchilada, please.	**C:** You, too.
C: Pretty good.	**W:** Wheat tortilla?	
	C: No, white's fine.	
	W: Here it is.	
	W: Is that all for you?	
	C: Yes, thanks.	

Many times, even in brief interactions, there is a beginning, middle, and end to the conversation. This is considered friendly and polite.

	Cafeteria Menu
Monday	**Soup:** Chicken Tortilla Soup $1.50 / $2.25 **Entrée:** Chicken Enchiladas $4.75 **Entrée:** Chicken Rice Bowl w/ Vegetable $3.79 **Sandwich:** Garlic Beef Melt w/French Fries $3.85 **Vegetables:** Mashed Potatoes, Broccoli, Carrots $0.75 each
Tuesday	**Soup:** French Onion Soup $1.50 / $2.25 **Entrée:** Chicken Burritos $4.75 **Entrée:** Chicken Rice Bowl w/Vegetable $3.79 **Sandwich:** Barbecued Turkey w/French Fries $3.85 **Vegetables:** Peas, Carrots, Mashed Potatoes $0.75 each
Wednesday	**Soup:** Garden Vegetable Soup $1.50 / $2.25 **Entrée:** Chipotle Beef w/Choice of Vegetable $4.50 **Entrée:** Jumbo Shrimp Fettuccine w/Garlic Bread $6.25 **Sandwich:** Turkey Melt w/French Fries $3.85 **Vegetables:** Mashed Potatoes, Cauliflower, Green Beans, Carrots $0.75 each
Thursday	**Soup:** Pasta and Beans $1.50 / $2.25 **Entrée:** Chili Verde w/Rice and Beans $4.50 **Entrée:** Garlic Peanut Chicken Wings w/Choice of Vegetable $4.75 **Sandwich:** Grilled Reuben w/French Fries $3.85 **Vegetables:** Mashed Potatoes, Broccoli, Carrots, Corn $0.75 each
Friday	**Soup:** New England Clam Chowder $1.50 / $2.25 **Entrée:** Baja Fish Tacos w/Rice and Beans $4.50 **Entrée:** Carne Asada w/Rice and Beans $4.50 **Sandwich:** Tuna Melt w/French Fries $3.85 **Vegetables:** Mashed Potatoes, Mixed Vegetables, Broccoli $0.75 each
Available daily	Sandwiches made to order Soup of the day Small fountain drink $3.99

Cultural Note   Cafeterias and fast-food restaurants are very busy places. They serve many people within a short amount of time. When it is your turn to order, you are expected to know what you want to order. If you have not decided by the time it is your turn, it's considered polite to let the person behind you go first while you finish deciding.

EVALUATION

ACTIVITY **A** Now that you have completed the activities in this chapter, complete the self-evaluation checklist below. Discuss your checklist with a classmate.

Self-Evaluation
Checklist

- ☐ I used expressions learned in this chapter to order food and take orders.
- ☐ I used rising and falling intonation correctly.
- ☐ I used less and more formal language correctly.
- ☐ I correctly identified complete sentences and sentences parts.
- ☐ My interactions had a beginning, a middle, and an end.
- ☐ I asked for repetition and spelling when necessary.
- ☐ I checked my understanding and confirmed information when necessary.
- ☐ I talked around words when necessary.
- ☐ I listed and understood the main ideas and details when listening.

ACTIVITY **B** Look back at the chapter and the self-evaluation checklist above. What can you do this week to improve the skills you have learned in this chapter? Talk with a partner and write an action plan for how you can improve your skills this week.

Example   *When I go to get food at the cafeteria or anywhere else, I'll listen to the "script" that the speaker uses to determine if I should use more or less formal language. I will then practice what I learned here to order my food. I will be sure that my interactions have a beginning, a middle, and an end.*

Action Plan

CHAPTER
5 | What's the Problem?

GET STARTED

 ACTIVITY **A**
CD 2 Track 17

Listen to three conversations. What is each person's problem? Write the answer below each picture.

a. _____   **b.** _____   **c.** _____

ACTIVITY **B**
Sometimes you have a problem that you need to explain. Match each item in the first column with an item in the second column. In some cases, more than one answer is possible.

1. I'm _____   **a.** very sick.

2. My mother _____   **b.** needs me.

3. I can't _____   **c.** isn't working.

4. I have _____   **d.** doesn't have the book I want.

5. My family _____   **e.** a terrible cold.

6. My computer _____   **f.** talk.

7. The bookstore _____ **g.** is at the hospital.

ACTIVITY **C**
Imagine that you are unable to keep an appointment or go to school or work. Write two possible reasons you might have.

1. _____

2. _____

LEARN AND PRACTICE

Explaining Problems with *Can* and *Can't*

In conversational English, the modal *can* and its negative form *can't* (*cannot*) are often used. *Can* is the third most common modal of the nine modal verbs in English. It is mostly used in conversation to express ability (or inability) and permission. *Can* and *can't* are often used when talking about problems.

◀)) ACTIVITY **A**   Listen to the conversation. Write the information you hear on the lines below.
CD 2 Track 18

> **A:** Hi, there.
>
> **B:** Hey.
>
> **A:** What's wrong? You look tired.
>
> **B:** Well, I . . . um . . . I _____ at night.
>   (a)
>
> **A:** Oh, I'm sorry to hear that.
>
> **B:** Yeah, I, um . . . I try to study, but I _____.
>   (b)
>
> **A:** That's terrible.
>
> **B:** Yeah.
>
> **A:** Have you tried seeing a doctor?
>
> **B:** I _____. I don't have health insurance.
>   (c)
>
> **A:** The school has a nurse.
>
> **B:** Really?
>
> **A:** Yes. He may be able to help you.
>
> **B:** That's a great idea. Where is his office?
>
> **A:** I _____ take you there right now if you want.
>   (d)
>
> **B:** Oh, that's so nice of you. Thanks.

GRAMMAR

The Modal *Can/Can't*

Use *can* and *can't* to express ability and inability in the present and the future.
Can and *can't* must be followed by the base form of the main verb.

| I | can | meet | you tomorrow afternoon. |

To form *can't*, contract *can* and *not*.

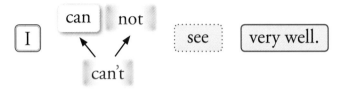

| I | can not | see | very well. |

can't

ACTIVITY **B**   **1.** Complete the boxes with things you can and cannot do sometimes.

I	can't	understand	what she says.
I	can't		
I	can		

2. Complete the boxes with things you can and cannot do tomorrow.

I	can't	study	with you.
I	can't		
I	can		

Word Stress and Pronunciation with *Can* and *Can't*

Sometimes it is difficult to hear the difference between *can* and *can't*, even for native speakers. It is also difficult to pronounce the differences between the two.

One difference is in the stress. When you say *can't*, you stress it. You make a louder and longer sound by opening your mouth wider. When you say *can*, you stress the verb after it. You do not open your mouth as wide when you say *can*.

Another difference is in the pronunciation. When *can* is followed by a verb in a sentence, *can* is pronounced *kn* (the vowel sound is dropped). However, the vowel sound in *can't* is always pronounced.

 Listen and repeat.

CD 2 Track 19

I **caaan't** see the picture.
I **caaan't** study with you tomorrow.

I c'n **see** it.
I c'n **go** to the gym at 10:00.

 ACTIVITY **C** Listen to the sentences. Write *can* or *can't* on each line below.

CD 2 Track 20

a. Tomorrow I _____ come to school at 9:00.

b. I _____ teach you that.

c. You _____ go to the gym for a while.

d. Your father _____ help you with that.

e. Ana _____ do that.

f. We _____ do that next year.

ACTIVITY **D** Your instructor will say things he or she can and can't do. Give a "thumbs down" if you hear *can't* and a "thumbs up" if you hear *can*.

ACTIVITY **E** Write down two things you can do and two things you can't do. Read the sentences to a partner. Can your partner hear the difference when you are saying *can* and when you are saying *can't*?

1. _____

2. _____

3. _____

4. _____

Using Modals for Suggestions

When we talk about problems, it is polite to offer a suggestion. We often use modals to make suggestions. Suggestions can be very soft or strong.

- *Can, could, may,* and *might want to* are used for soft suggestions. These modals tell the listener that he or she can follow your suggestions if he or she wants to. The advice is optional.

- *Need to* and *have got to* are verbs that work like modals (semi-modals) and are used to express stronger suggestions. These modals warn the listener that if he or she does not take your advice, there will be a negative result.

Sentence Structure

Sentence structure in English usually is Subject + Verb + Complement.
Not all sentences have a complement. When a modal is added, the structure
becomes Subject + Verb (modal + base form) + Complement.

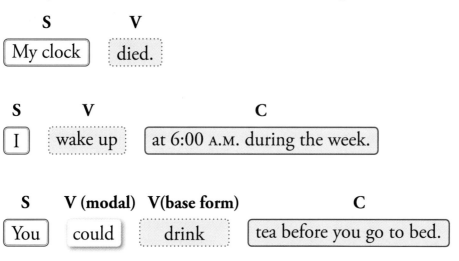

ACTIVITY **F** **1.** Read the suggestions for someone who cannot sleep at night. Notice the
sentence structure: Subject + Verb (Modal + Base Form) + Complement.

2. Write down two strong suggestions and two soft suggestions for someone who cannot sleep at night.

    a. Strong suggestion: _____

    b. Strong suggestion: _____

    c. Soft suggestion: _____

    d. Soft suggestion: _____

🔊 ACTIVITY **G**   Listen to two conversations and answer the questions.

CD 2 Track 21

CONVERSATION 1

    a. What's the problem? _____

    b. What are the suggestions? _____

    c. Are the suggestions soft or strong? _____

CONVERSATION 2

    a. What's the problem? _____

    b. What are the suggestions? _____

    c. Are the suggestions soft or strong? _____

ACTIVITY **H**   Write a suggestion for each of the problems in the chart. Then circle *1, 2, 3, 4,* or *5* (*1* is very soft and *5* is very strong) depending on how strong you think the suggestion is. Discuss your choices with a partner.

Problem	Suggestions	Strong or Soft?
I can't sleep well at night. I have anxiety problems.		**1 - 2 - 3 - 4 - 5**
I don't like my sister's boyfriend. I can't tell my sister though. She's going to be angry with me.		**1 - 2 - 3 - 4 - 5**
I have a toothache, but I can't see a dentist. I have no money.		**1 - 2 - 3 - 4 - 5**

Speaking Politely: Conversations with a Beginning, a Middle, and an End

Polite conversations generally have a sequence that includes a beginning, a middle, and an end. Conversations about problems include these three parts.

Beginning: Opening Greeting

A: Hi, there.
B: Hey.
A: What's wrong? You look tired?

Middle: Explaining the Problem and Offering a Suggestion

B: Well, I . . . um . . . I can't sleep at night.
A: Oh, I'm sorry to hear that.
B: Yeah, I, um . . . I try to study, but I can't concentrate.   } Explaining the Problem
A: That's terrible.
B: Yeah.

A: You might want to see a doctor.
B: I don't have health insurance.
A: The school has a nurse.   } Offering a Suggestion
B: Really?
A: Yes. Maybe he can help you.

B: That's a great idea. I'll go see him right now.   } Responding to the Suggestion

OR

B: The nurse isn't there when I can go see him.   } Accepting or Rejecting the Suggestion

End: Final Comments / Closing Greeting / Saying Good-bye

A: I hope you feel better.
B: Thanks. Me, too.

ACTIVITY
CD 2 Track 22

1. Listen to the conversation. One student has a problem, and other students are giving suggestions.

2. Work in a small group. Choose a problem from the list below or use a problem of your own. Take turns explaining your problem to your group. Your group members will give you suggestions. Accept or reject each suggestion. Make sure the conversations have a beginning, a middle, and an end. Use the expressions below to help you.

Problems

- I live in an apartment that I really like. I'd hate to move, but my rent is much more expensive now than when I moved in. I can't afford it.

- My sister and her two children are coming to visit us. The problem is that my husband, our son, and I live in a small two-bedroom apartment. I can't tell my sister that they should stay at a hotel because she might think that it is very rude.

- I have a very difficult job. My boss is very demanding, and she makes me very nervous. I can't sleep at night worrying about going to work the next day.

- I love my friend Veronica. She and I are taking some classes together. Veronica always wants us to study together. The problem is that I can't focus when I study with her. She always starts talking about other things.

- When I lived in my country, I had a maid. Now I have to do household chores myself. The problem is I can't cook at all, and I have no interest in learning how to cook. I have put on 12 pounds eating junk food.

Useful Expressions

> I think you need to . . .
> I really think you've got to . . .

> That's a good idea.

> Hmm, I'll think about it.

GRAMMAR

The Present Progressive Tense

Use the present progressive tense to describe problems that are happening now.
Use *be* + verb with *-ing* (present participle).

| It | isn't | working. |
| It | is | leaking. |

ACTIVITY **J**   Match each verb with the appropriate object. Write the verb below the picture.

| connect | dry | write | make ice | start |

_____   _____   _____

_____   _____

GRAMMAR

Explaining Problems with the Present Progressive Tense

The present progressive is frequently used to explain problems with objects at the moment they are happening.

ACTIVITY **K**   Write the problem with each of the objects from Activity J. Use the present progressive tense.

a. My computer _____

b. My pen _____

c. My dryer _____

d. My refrigerator _____

e. My car _____

ACTIVITY **L** What is the problem with each object? Write a sentence about the problem with each item. Use a verb from the box and the present progressive tense. Use each verb once.

show the time	boot up	work	vibrate

_____

_____

_____

_____

_____

_____

_____

_____

Making Requests Using *Can*

When you have a problem, use questions with *can* to ask for help.

Problem: My pen isn't working.

Request: Can │ I │ borrow │ a pen?

Problem: I don't understand the homework assignment.

Request: Can │ you │ help │ me?

ACTIVITY **M** Work with a partner. Take turns explaining a problem you are having with one of the objects below. Use the present progressive to explain your problem. Then use *can* to request help.

cell phone   pen   pencil   eraser   calculator   electronic dictionary   (your own idea)

Cultural Note   It is acceptable to ask strangers for favors that do not inconvenience them too much, such as asking for the time, for directions, or to borrow a pen. However, it is not usually okay to ask for money or to use a personal object, such as a cell phone.

REVIEW: GRAMMAR

Expressing Problems with the Simple Present Tense, the Present Progressive Tense, and *Can't*

You can use the simple present, the present progressive, and *can't* to talk about problems.

ACTIVITY **N** In each conversation below, people are explaining problems. Write the type of verb (simple present, present progressive) or modal (*can't*) the speaker is using.

CONVERSATION 1

A: What are you doing?
B: Fixing my phone.
A: What's wrong with it?
B: It isn't ringing loud enough. _____

CONVERSATION 2

A: You look tired.
B: I have a test tomorrow, and I can't relax. _____
A: Come on! You know you're a good student.
B: Thanks.

CONVERSATION 3

A: Dr. Kim?

B: Speaking.

A: Hi, this is Carmen Velasco, um . . . from your English 71 class?

B: Hi, Carmen. How are you?

A: All right. I'm sorry, I can't go to school today _____
because I'm running a temperature. _____
I think I have a bad cold. _____

B: Sorry to hear that.

A: Can I take the test some other day?

B: How about Monday at 9:00?

A: Sounds good. Thanks so much.

ACTIVITY **O**   For each problem, write a question asking for help.

a. Problem: My pencil sharpener isn't working.
   Request: _____

b. Problem: I don't have a notebook.
   Request: _____

c. Problem: I can't remember my password.
   Request: _____

d. Problem: My scissors aren't cutting.
   Request: _____

REVIEW: LISTENING STRATEGIES

Listening for the Main Idea

When you listen for the main idea, create a mental picture of what is happening.
After you listen, answer the questions.

 ACTIVITY **P**
CD 2 Track 23

1. Listen to two conversations. Use the strategy for listening for the main idea from the box above.

2. After listening to the conversations, discuss these questions with your classmates:

   • What objects are the people talking about?
   • What's the problem with the objects?

Listening for Details

When you listen for details, you need to do things before, during, and after the listening task. Before listening, preview the questions you need to answer. Then take brief notes as you listen. After the listening, read your notes and use the information to answer the questions.

🔊 ACTIVITY **Q**
CD 2 Track 24

1. Listen to the two conversations again. Use the strategies for listening to details from the box above.

2. After listening to the conversations, answer the questions below.

   a. Conversation 1:

   What is the name and telephone number of the person with the problem?

   _____

   When will the object be ready for pick up? _____

   b. Conversation 2:

   What is the name and telephone number of the person with the problem?

   _____

   When will the object be ready for pick up? _____

ACTIVITY **R**   Complete the conversations below with your own words.

CONVERSATION 1

   A: Mia?
   B: Yes
   A: My pen isn't working. _____?
   B: Sorry. _____.
   A: That's all right.

CONVERSATION 2

   A: Do you have a pencil I can borrow?
   B: _____. Here it is.
   A: _____.

CONVERSATION 3

   A: Sorry to bother you . . .
   B: Huh?
   A: _____. Can I use your _____?
   B: Sorry, _____.
   A: Oh, that's all right. _____.

Speaking Politely: Negative Responses to Requests

When you talk, it is very important to be polite. When someone asks a favor, it sounds impolite to just say, "No." Instead, say, "Sorry," or "I'm sorry," and then give a brief explanation. Giving a brief explanation makes you sound more polite. If you made the request, always say, "Thank you," even if the answer was negative. This shows that you are polite and that the person did not have an obligation to help you.

ACTIVITY **S** Read the conversation below. Then discuss these questions with your classmates: Which speakers are polite and which are not? How do you know?

Conversation 1	Conversation 2
A: Could you do me a quick favor?	**A:** Could I ask you a favor?
B: What is it?	**B:** Sure.
A: Could you lend me a pair of scissors?	**A:** Can I use your cell phone real quick?
B: No.	**B:** I'm sorry. My cell phone just died.
	A: That's all right. Thanks anyway.

ACTIVITY **T** **1.** For each type of verb, write a problem using that verb type. Then ask for help using the modal *can*.

	Problem	Request
Simple present		
Present progressive		
Can't		

CD 2 Track 25

2. Listen to a student telling a classmate about a problem and making a request.

3. Go around the classroom. Tell a classmate about one of the problems in the chart from Step 1 and make the request in the chart. Be sure your conversation has a beginning, a middle, and an end. Remember to use polite language. Repeat with a different classmate for the other two problems and requests in the chart.

REVIEW AND EXPAND

ACTIVITY **A** Choose an object from the list below. Get up and walk around the classroom. Tell a classmate a problem you are having with the object and make a request. Be sure your conversation has a beginning, a middle, and an end. Repeat with two other objects and classmates.

> pen   pencil   electronic dictionary   eraser   calculator   scissors

Remember to...
- include a beginning, a middle, and an end in your conversation.
- explain the problem.
- ask for help.
- respond. Do not just say, "No." Say, "Sorry," or "I'm sorry," and give a brief explanation.
- thank the person for considering your request. If the answer is no, say, "That's all right," "That's OK," or "Thanks anyway."

ACTIVITY **B** Work in pairs. Choose a situation below. Create a conversation about the situation. Perform your conversation in front of the class. Your classmates must guess which situation the conversation is about.

Situation 1: You are telling a friend about a problem you are having with an object. Your friend will give you a suggestion. Accept it.

Situation 2: You are telling a family member or friend about something you cannot do. Ask for help.

Situation 3: You are at a repair shop explaining what is wrong with an object you own.

EVALUATION

ACTIVITY A   Now that you have completed the activities in this chapter, complete the self-evaluation checklist below. Discuss your checklist with a classmate.

Self-Evaluation
Checklist

- ☐ I explained my problems with the simple present, present progressive, or *can't*.
- ☐ I pronounced *can* and *can't* correctly.
- ☐ I offered suggestions correctly.
- ☐ My conversations had a beginning, a middle, and an end.
- ☐ I used *can* to make requests.
- ☐ I spoke politely when I said "no" to a request.
- ☐ I built mental pictures when listening for the main idea.
- ☐ I listened and understood the main ideas and details.
- ☐ I asked for repetition and spelling when necessary.
- ☐ I checked my understanding and confirmed information when necessary.

ACTIVITY B   Look back at the chapter and the self-evaluation checklist above. What can you do this week to improve the skills you have learned in this chapter? Talk with a partner and write an action plan for how you can improve your skills this week.

Example   **I need to work on using "I'm sorry" instead of "no" when responding to a request. I always use "no" first. I'm going to practice by creating conversations, making sure that I use "I'm sorry," and then giving a reason. I'm also going to talk in English with my friends so that I can practice when we chat.**

Action Plan

GET STARTED

 ACTIVITY **A**
CD 2 Track 26

Listen to three conversations. In each conversation, a person is making a phone call. Answer the questions below.

CONVERSATION 1

    a. Is the person calling work or school? _____

    b. What is the person's problem? _____

CONVERSATION 2

    a. Is the person calling work or school? _____

    b. What is the person's problem? _____

CONVERSATION 3

    a. Is the person calling work or school? _____

    b. What is the person's problem? _____

ACTIVITY **B**
Sometimes you are not able to go to work or school. Write three reasons why you are sometimes unable to go to work or school.

1. I have a bad cold. _____

2. _____

3. _____

4. _____

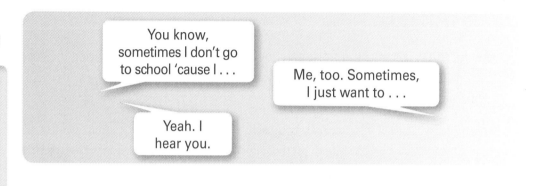

ACTIVITY **C**
CD 2 Track 27

1. Listen to a group of students talk about why they sometimes don't go to work or school.

2. In groups of three or four, discuss the reasons why you sometimes don't go to work or school.

Useful *Expressions*

I hear you means that you understand and can sympathize with the person's experience.

> You know, sometimes I don't go to school 'cause I . . .

> Me, too. Sometimes, I just want to . . .

> Yeah. I hear you.

LEARN AND PRACTICE

REVIEW: GRAMMAR

Explaining Problems

In Chapter 5, you learned how to express inability with *can't*. You also learned to use *can't* to talk about problems in the present and future.

 ACTIVITY **A**
CD 2 Track 28

Listen to each conversation. Near the end of the conversation, the narrator will ask a question. During the pause, circle the answer to the question. Then listen to the rest of the conversation to check your answer.

CONVERSATION 1

Why can't the man go to school this week?

a. He can't eat well.

b. He can't drive.

c. He can't concentrate.

CONVERSATION 2

What do you think the woman can't do today?

a. She can't go to work today.

b. She can't cook today.

c. She can't study today.

What do you think Mira will say she can't do?

a. She can't go to the coffee shop.

b. She can't talk on the phone.

c. She can't see the road.

GRAMMAR

Expressing Obligation, Desire, and Future Plans

When you have a problem and need to give an explanation, you can talk about things you have to do (**obligation**), things you want to do (**desire**), or things you plan to do (**future plans**).

Expressing Obligation

An obligation is something you have to do.

I | need to / have to / have got to / 've got to | take | my son to the doctor today.

Have to is very common in spoken English; *have got to* is somewhat common.

ACTIVITY **B**   Complete the sentences below with obligations you have next week. Follow the example.

Example   I can't come to class next Monday *because I have to see my doctor.*

1. I can't go to work on Friday because _____

2. I can't come to school next week because _____

GRAMMAR

Expressing Desire

A desire is something you want to do. Sometimes we cannot agree to a request because we simply *want to* or *would like to* do something else.

I | would like to | go | to a movie this weekend.

ACTIVITY **C**   Complete the sentences below with things you want to do next week. Follow the example.

Example   I can't meet you on Friday because <u>I want to go to the gym.</u>

1. I can't play soccer with you on Monday because _____
2. I can't see the movie Saturday night because _____

GRAMMAR

Expressing Future Plans

Sometimes we cannot do something because we already have future plans.

| I | 'm going to | study | for a test. |

Be going to is extremely common in conversations, but it is rare in formal writing.

ACTIVITY **D**   Complete the sentences below with things you plan to do next week. Follow the example.

Example   I can't give you a ride to school on Friday because <u>I'm going to take a driving test.</u>

1. I can't go to the gym with you tomorrow because _____
2. I can't study with you on Saturday because _____

ACTIVITY **E**   Circle the expressions of time that indicate future.

every day	when I was a child	on my birthday last year
tomorrow	later	in a minute
next week	this morning	after class today
in a second	tonight	this afternoon (It's 6:00 P.M.)
later today	always	every year on my birthday
yesterday	every morning	next year on my birthday
		when I turn 45 (I'm 20 now.)

◀)) ACTIVITY F
CD 2 Track 29

Listen to three conversations. In each conversation, the person cannot go to work or school. Is the person's reason an obligation, a desire, or future plans? Circle the correct answer. You may circle more than one option in some conversations.

Conversation 1:	obligation	desire	future plans
Conversation 2:	obligation	desire	future plans
Conversation 3:	obligation	desire	future plans

ACTIVITY G

We can also express obligation, desire, or future plans to explain why we need somebody's help when we make a request or ask a favor. Tell a classmate what you are going to do Saturday morning. Request help from him or her using *can*.

Example   **A:** Can you help me study for my math test on Saturday morning?
I'm going to study for my test then, but I don't understand the material.
B: I'm so sorry, Andy, but on Saturday morning I've got to study for a writing test I have on Monday.
A: Oh, that's OK. Thanks anyway.

Cultural Note   When we ask people for a favor that requires their time, we need to give a good reason. Time is considered precious. Remember, time is money!

◀)) ACTIVITY H
CD 2 Track 30

Listen to the conversations. What is each person's reason—obligation, desire, or future plans—for making a request? Circle the correct answer.

Conversation 1:	obligation	desire	future plans
Conversation 2:	obligation	desire	future plans
Conversation 3:	obligation	desire	future plans

◀)) ACTIVITY I
CD 2 Track 31

Listen to the conversations again. Does each person get what he or she asked for? Circle *yes*, *no*, or *not clear*.

Conversation 1:	yes	no	not clear
Conversation 2:	yes	no	not clear
Conversation 3:	yes	no	not clear

ACTIVITY **J** Work in groups of three or four. Choose one student to be the secretary. (The secretary is the only one who can record your group's answers.) Your instructor will give you the first part of a sentence that tells about a problem. For example: *I can't turn in my project on Friday because* . . . Your group will have two minutes to complete the sentence with as many reasons as you can think of. The secretary will write down the group's answers.

For each round, use a different type of reason:

Round 1: Use reasons that express **obligation**.

Round 2: Use reasons that express **desire**.

Round 3: Use reasons that express **future plans**.

Final Round: Your instructor will choose one of the problems below. You have three minutes to write as many excuses as possible. This time you have to use all of the following: an **obligation**, **desire**, and **future plans**. The winner is the group that has the most correct sentences at the end of the final round.

Problems:

1. I can't come to work next Monday because . . .

2. I can't come on the day of the test because . . .

3. I can't go to your birthday party because . . .

4. I can't study with you tomorrow because . . .

 ACTIVITY **K**
CD 2 Track 32

1. Listen to the conversation. One speaker is asking the other speaker for a favor.

2. Work with a partner. Role-play a situation in which you ask your partner for a favor. Follow the steps below. Then switch roles.

Speaker A	⟶	Greet Speaker B.
Speaker B	⟶	Respond.
Speaker A	⟶	Ask for a favor. Tell what you need help with and when you need it.
Speaker B	⟶	Tell Speaker A that you cannot help. Use an obligation, a desire, or future plans to explain why.

Reduced Form (Reductions)

CD 2 Track 33

Sometimes spoken English seems very fast and is difficult to understand. However, the actual speed of the speech is not usually very fast. What makes it sound fast is that many words are not pronounced individually. Many words are pronounced together, and they sound like one word. These are called *reductions*.

For example:

Full Form		Reduced Form
I **have to** study.		I *hafta* study.
I've **got to** work.	⟶	I've *gotta* work. OR I *gotta* work.
I **want to** rest. He **wants to** rest.		I *wanna* rest. He *wantzta* rest.
I'm **going to** exercise.		I'm *gonna* exercise.

Note: Reduced forms are only used in speech. Reduced forms are generally not used in academic or formal writing.

 ACTIVITY **L**   Listen to the conversation. Circle the form (full or reduced) that you hear.

CD 2 Track 34

A: Dr. Chang's office. How can I help you?

B: Mira? This is Liz Santos.

A: Hi, Ms. Santos. How's the baby?

B: Oh, he's doing very well, thanks. He's **(going to / gonna)** start walking any minute.

A: Ohhhh! Does he eat everything already?

B: Almost. He **(wants to / wantzta)** eat everything we eat, but . . . uh . . . you know.

A: Yep, I do. Well, what can I do for you?

B: Oh, I have an appointment with Dr. Chang in a week, but I've **(got to / gotta)** leave town on Sunday. I have a conference to go to.

A: Well, let me see his schedule.

B: Thanks.

A: How about . . . um . . . let me see . . . a week after that at 9:00?

B: I can't in the morning. I've **(got to / gotta)** work.

A: OK, then. How about the 5th at 3 P.M.?

B: Oh, sorry, on that day I'm **(going to / gonna)** . . . hold on . . . oh, here it is. . . . I **(have to / hafta)** go to a meeting downtown.

A: OK, that's tough. Let me see . . .

CD 2 Track 35

1. Listen to a person explaining a problem. Listen for the reduced forms in the conversation.

2. You are going to work in pairs. First, practice aloud the full forms and reduced forms from the chart on page 91. Then Student A will explain a problem to Student B. Remember to use *hafta, gotta, wanna, gonna* and other reduced forms in your conversation.

REVIEW: GRAMMAR

Making Polite Requests

When we explain problems at school or work, we usually ask for something. This is called *making a request*. We use *"Can I"* to make polite requests.

For example:

Can I
- talk — to you in your office tomorrow?
- leave — ten minutes early today?
- come — in late tomorrow?

CD 2 Track 36

Listen to each conversation. Near the end of the conversation, the narrator will ask a question. Write your answer on the lines below. Then listen to the rest of the conversation to check your answer.

Conversation 1: _____

Conversation 2: _____

Conversation 3: _____

ACTIVITY **0**   Work in a group of three or four. Your instructor will tape sheets of paper on the wall around the classroom. Follow the steps below.

Step 1: Get a marker (one marker per group) and stand in front of a sheet of paper.

Step 2: Your instructor will give you a problem from the chart below. With your group, decide the request you would make if you had that problem. Then write the request on the sheet of paper.

Step 3: Move to the next sheet of paper on your right. Read the request that the previous group wrote. Check if the grammar is correct and if it makes sense. If there are any mistakes, correct them.

Step 4: Repeat Steps 2 and 3 until you come back to the same sheet of paper you started with.

Place	Problem
1. at school	I have a doctor's appointment on the day of the test.
2. at work	My mom is going to have emergency surgery on Friday, but I have no sick days left.
3. at school	I have to go back home for two weeks. My dad is very ill, so I won't be here for the meeting about the project.
4. at work	I'm going to get married next month, but I don't have any more vacation time left.
5. at school	I've got to have my wisdom teeth removed tomorrow, so I can't teach my afternoon class.
6. at work	I have to renew my driver's license on Tuesday, so I have to leave early on that day.
7. at work	I can't come to work on Wednesday next week because I'm going to move out of my apartment.

Cultural Note   To avoid a conflict in schedule, make sure that you make arrangements as far in advance as possible (a week or more). It is sometimes considered inappropriate to try to make arrangements the day before.

Using *So* and *Then*

So and *then* are extremely common linking words in conversational English. They help you connect ideas when you are explaining something.

Using *So*

So can be used to connect a problem you have to a request. State the reason or problem and then use *so* as a transition to your request for help.

Reason/Problem	*So*	Request
I can't come to school tomorrow,	so	can I take the test on Monday?
I've got to go to the DMV on Monday,	so	can I turn in my homework on Tuesday?
I want to talk to the counselor,	so	can I meet you a little later?

So can also begin a request for help or a favor.

Reason/Problem	*So* + Request
I'm going to study for a test.	**So,** can we see a movie another day?
I've got to work this evening.	**So,** can we meet for dinner tomorrow night?

ACTIVITY **P**   Read each reason or problem. Then write a request beginning with *so*.

a. I need to go to the library tomorrow afternoon, but I don't have a car.

   Request: _____

b. I'm going to study for the math exam, and I know you're good at math.

   Request: _____

c. I don't want to eat in the cafeteria tomorrow. It's Friday!

   Request: _____

d. I've got to interview someone for my speaking class.

   Request: _____

Using *Then*

Then is often used with a suggestion.

Problem	Suggestion	*then*
I can't come to school tomorrow, so I can't bring my homework assignment.	Bring it on Tuesday	**then**.
I want to talk to the counselor at 11:00.	Leave five minutes early today	**then**.
I need to study for my test, but I don't understand the simple present.	Ask a classmate for help	**then**.

Then can also begin a suggestion.

Problem	*Then* + Suggestion
I can't come to school tomorrow, so I can't bring my homework assignment.	**Then** bring it on Tuesday.
I want to talk to the counselor at 11:00.	**Then** leave five minutes early today.
I need to study for my test, but I don't understand the simple present.	**Then** ask a classmate for help.

ACTIVITY **Q**   Read each problem. Write a suggestion using *then*.

a. I can't find my friend's telephone number.

Suggestion: _____

b. I need to improve my listening.

Suggestion: _____

c. I have to study, but I can't find time.

Suggestion: _____

d. I want to go to the beach, but I don't have a car.

Suggestion: _____

ACTIVITY **R**   Complete the conversations below with *so* or *then*.

CONVERSATION 1

    A: Mr. Petris?

    B: Yes?

    A: May I talk to you?

    B: Sure. Come on in. How can I help you?

    A: Well, I um, um . . . I'm having a problem. . . .

    B: Uh-huh.

    A: I have jury duty tomorrow.

    B: Uh-huh.

    A: _____, . . . I was wondering . . .
              (a)

    B: Yes?

    A: Can I take the test the day after tomorrow?

    B: Um, can you be here an hour early?

    A: I can do that. In your office or in the classroom?

    B: Here . . . in my office.

    A: I'll be here at 9:00. Thanks a lot.

    B: Sure. Leave early _____, traffic is horrible at that time.
                           (b)

    A: I will. Thanks.

CONVERSATION 2

    A: Ms. Ferreira?

    B: Yes?

    A: Hi, I, um, I need to talk to you.

    B: Sure. What's the problem?

    A: Well, I, um, I'm having difficulty with my homework.

    B: Oh, I see.

    A: I don't really understand what I'm doing wrong.

    B: Do you have time to go to the writing center?

    A: Yes.

    B: Go to the writing center _____
                       (c)

    A: OK.

    B: And ask the tutor there to help you.

> *Jury duty* is when one has to go to a court of law to serve on the jury for a trial.

A: _____, can I turn in the homework tomorrow instead?
  _(d)

B: Sure.

A: Oh, that's great. Thanks a lot.

B: All right, then.

ACTIVITY **S**

1. Work in groups of four. Use the problem and solution cards from pages 175–176.

2. Place the problem cards face down in a pile.

3. Divide the solution cards between your group members. Each student displays the solution cards on the desk so everybody can see them.

4. The first student starts by picking a problem card. This student has to explain his or her problem to the group.

5. The other group members check their solution cards. If you think one of the solutions fits the problem, make a suggestion using *then*.

6. If the solution makes sense, the student with the problem accepts the suggestion by saying, "That's a great idea. Thanks." If it does not make sense, or if it is not a good suggestion, the student politely rejects the suggestion and gives a brief explanation by saying, "I'm sorry. I don't think that'll work."

7. Take turns picking up a problem card until all the problem cards have been used.

REVIEW AND EXPAND

ACTIVITY **A**   Most conversations follow a general sequence that includes a beginning, a middle, and an end. Conversations in which a person explains a problem and asks a favor also follow a sequence. Read the conversation below. Identify the parts of the conversations and write the answers on the lines.

Getting permission to talk	Introducing the problem
Asking for a favor	Granting / not granting a favor
Saying thank you/good-bye	Getting the person's attention

A: Ms. Santana? ⎱
B: Yes? ⎰ _____ (a)

A: <u>Do you have a minute?</u> ⎱
B: Sure. Come on in. ⎰ _____ (b)

A: OK, well . . .

B: How can I help you?

A: I, um, <u>I have a problem.</u>

B: Ok.

A: I, . . . um, I have to go to Korea for two weeks.

B: Two weeks?

A: Yeah, I, um . . . my dad is ill . . .

B: Uh-huh.

A: <u>My mom wants us all there.</u>

                     }   _____ (c)

B: I see.

A: So, I was wondering . . .

B: Uh-huh.

A: Can I miss two weeks of classes?

                     }   _____ (d)

B: Well, that's a tough one.

A: I know.

B: OK, look, I . . . let me check your grades.

A: Uh-huh.

B: <u>You're doing very well this semester</u> . . .

A: Uh-huh, thanks.

B: And <u>you don't have any absences or missed assignments</u> . . .

A: Uh-huh.

B: So, you can go . . .

A: Oh, thanks a lot.

B: And I'll give you the test when you come back.

                     }   _____ (e)

A: That sounds great. Thanks.

B: You have to do the online assignments while you're there, though.

A: Sure, that won't be a problem.

B: Good. So, good luck, and I hope your dad gets better.

A: <u>Thanks so much, Ms. Santana.</u> } _____ (f)

ACTIVITY **B**   Read the conversation again. Discuss with a partner which verb tense is used in the underlined sentences—the simple present or the present progressive?

1. Imagine that you have a problem you need to tell your instructor. In the box below, write a problem you have. Use inability, desire, obligation, or future plans to explain your problem.

Problem

_____

_____

2. In the box below, write the favor you will ask your instructor.

Favor

Can I _____

_____

3. In each box below, write part of the conversation between you and your instructor about the problem you have.

Part 1

Your instructor is leaving the classroom. Get his or her attention and politely ask to talk to him or her.

You:

Part 2

Introduce your problem (use present tense, inability, desire, obligation or future plans). Write the instructor's questions, too.

You:

 Your teacher:

Part 3

Use *so* and ask the favor.

You:

Part 4

Your instructor will grant you the favor or not. Your teacher may also make a suggestion (use *then*).

Your teacher:

Part 5

Thank your instructor (even if the answer was negative) and say good-bye.

You:

ACTIVITY **D** Work with a partner. Role-play a conversation between a student and an instructor. Decide roles and follow the guidelines for each role below. (Remember: This is a role-play. Do not read the conversations parts you wrote in Activity C.) Use the speaking strategies and grammar points on the next page to help you.

Student A: You are a student, and you have a problem. Your instructor is in his or her office. Knock on the door, ask for permission to talk to him or her, explain your problem, and ask for the favor. Use *so* to connect a favor to the reason you are asking it.

Student B: You are an instructor. You are in your office when a student knocks on the door and asks to talk to you about a problem. Listen and ask questions. Use *then* to offer a suggestion.

Remember to . . .	• ask for repetition.	→	Excuse me? Could you say that again, please?
	• ask for spelling.	→	Can/could you spell that, please?
	• check your understanding.	→	You said . . . ?
	• confirm information.	→	That's right! / Yes! / That's correct.

- use *have to, need to*, and *have got to* to express obligation or *can't* to express inability.
- use *want to* to express desire.
- use *be going to* to express future plans.

EVALUATION

ACTIVITY A Now that you have completed the activities in this chapter, complete the self-evaluation checklist below. Discuss your checklist with a classmate.

Self-Evaluation Checklist

☐ I was able to explain my problem.

I used the following structures to explain my problem. (Circle all that apply.)

Present Tense   Inability   Desire   Obligation   Future Plans

☐ I used reduced forms when I spoke.
☐ I made polite requests.
☐ I connected my thoughts with *so* and *then*.
☐ I asked for repetition, spelling, and clarification when necessary.
☐ I checked and confirmed information when necessary.
☐ I made sure that my conversations had a beginning, a middle, and an end.

ACTIVITY B Look back at the chapter and the self-evaluation checklist above. What can you do this week to improve the skills you have learned in this chapter? Talk with a partner. Turn to the next page and write an action plan for how you can improve your skills this week.

Example I need to work on listening for reduced forms and using reduced forms when I speak. I'm going to use the Internet to listen and learn more reduced forms. I'll practice listening to them on the Internet, and I'll also watch one hour of TV in English. I'll practice using reduced forms when I talk with other people.

Action Plan

GET STARTED

🔊 ACTIVITY **A**   Listen to two conversations and answer the questions.
CD 3 Track 1

CONVERSATION 1

    a. When did the woman go to the restaurant?

    b. How was the experience?

    c. Had the woman and the man been there before?

    d. Is the woman going there again any time soon?

CONVERSATION 2

    a. Where did the woman go?

    b. How was the experience?

    c. What did the woman order?

    d. What was the problem with the order?

ACTIVITY **B**   It is common to ask others about their weekend. Think about your past weekend. What did you do? Check the activities you did and write two more things you did.

_____ saw a movie	_____ watched television
_____ stayed home	_____ went to a party
_____ studied	_____
_____ worked	_____

 ACTIVITY **C**
CD 3 Track 2

1. Listen to two students talk about their weekends.

2. Write down the verbs used to express what the student did.

LEARN AND PRACTICE

Simple Past Tense

In previous chapters, you learned to speak in the present and future. Now, you will focus on the past.

The simple past is used to express actions that happened in the past. We can often identify the tense (past, present, or future) by looking at the time expressions.

ACTIVITY **A**   Look at the time expressions below. In pairs, write if they express the past, present, or future tense.

sometimes _____   on my last vacation _____

tomorrow _____   next year on my birthday _____

every day _____   a second ago _____

in a minute _____   when I finish college _____

last year _____   when I was little _____

never _____   every year on my birthday _____

        when I turn 21 (I'm 19 now.) _____

ACTIVITY **B**   Stand next to your desk. Your instructor will call out time expressions. If it expresses:

- the **present**, jump up and down in place.

- the **past**, take one step back.

- the **future**, take one step forward.

Time Expressions		
a minute ago	usually	every other day
in a day	every Saturday	every summer
on my next birthday	next Saturday	last summer
last year on my birthday	in a second	

ACTIVITY **C**   When you speak, it is possible to use all the tenses in one conversation. Read the conversation below. Identify the tense of the parts of the conversation in brackets. Write *present*, *past*, or *future* on the line.

A: Oh, gosh, guess what happened yesterday.
B: What?   _____ (a)

A: Well, you know that Japanese restaurant across the street?
B: Uh-huh.
A: Well, um, I went there last night.
B: OK.
A: And, well, I ordered some sushi and sashimi.
B: Yeah?
A: And it, um, well, it looked good, but it all tasted awful.
B: Really?
A: Uh-huh. You know, I always go to that restaurant   _____ (b)

B: I know. I went there last week with you.   _____ (c)

A: So, I always go there, and it's always good . . .   _____ (d)

B: It was good when I went with you.   _____ (e)

A: I know!
B: Well, maybe last night was an isolated incident.   _____ (f)

A: I hope so 'cause I'm gonna go there again
next week with my boss.   _____ (g)
B: I'm sure it's gonna be alright.

A: I hope so.

Gosh is an expression associated with pleasant and unpleasant ideas. In conversation, *gosh* is often used to show surprise. "God," "My God," and "Gosh" are extremely frequent expressions in conversational English.

Simple Past Tense: Statements

The simple past tense is used to talk about events that happened (started and ended) at a specific time in the past. Study the forms of the verbs below.

Simple Present Tense

| I | eat out | once a week. |

Simple Past Tense

| I | ate out | once a week. |

There are two types of verbs in English: regular and irregular. Study the chart below. What is the difference between regular and irregular verbs?

Regular Verbs		Irregular Verbs	
Base Form	**Simple Past**	**Base Form**	**Simple Past**
dance	danc**ed**	go	**went**
look	look**ed**	take	**took**
study	stud**ied**	drink	**drank**

Regular Verbs

Follow these rules to form the simple past tense of regular verbs.

- If the verb ends in a consonant, add *-ed* to the end of the verb.
- If the verb ends in an *e,* add *-d* to the end of the verb.
- If the verb ends in a consonant + *y* (such as *study*), drop the *y* and add *-ied* (*studied*).
- If the verb ends in a vowel + *y* (such as *play*), just add *-ed* (*played*).

Irregular Verbs

The form of irregular verbs in the simple past tense must be memorized. There are no rules for these irregular forms.

ACTIVITY **D**   Remember that the simple past tense expresses an action that happened in the past and is finished. Read the conversation below. Discuss if the conversation is about a past, present, or future action. Discuss which verbs are regular and which are irregular.

> **A:** How was your weekend?
> **B:** Well, not so great. I didn't have much money to do what I wanted.
> **A:** What did you want to do?
> **B:** Go shopping.
> **A:** Oh.
> **B:** Yeah. I wanted to buy some stuff I saw at Becky's . . .
> **A:** Uh-huh?
> **B:** But, you know, I had no money, so . . .
> **A:** Well, maybe next month then.
> **B:** I guess.

ACTIVITY **E**   **1.** You are going to practice irregular past tense verbs with your classmates. Form two circles, with an equal number of students in each—an outside circle and an inside circle. Each student in the outside circle must stand facing a student in the inside circle.

CD 3 Track 3

2. Before you begin, listen to a pair of students completing the activity on irregular simple past tense forms.

3. Your instructor will give you some play money or coins and ask you to keep score as you go along. Follow the steps in the chart below.

Students in the Inside Circle	Students in the Outside Circle
• Open your books.	• Close your books.
• Choose a verb from the chart on the next page.	• Your partner will say the base form of an irregular verb.
• Say the base form of the verb to your partner.	• Say the simple past tense form of the verb.
• Your partner must say the simple past tense form of the verb.	• If your answer is wrong, you must give your partner one dollar in play money (or one coin). If the answer is correct, nothing is given.
• If your partner's answer is wrong, he or she must give you one dollar in play money (or one coin). If the answer is correct, nothing is given.	

4. When your instructor calls "Switch!," the students in the inside circle close their books and the students in the outside circle open their books. Then the outside circle students will test the inside circle students.

Base Form	Simple Past	Base Form	Simple Past
say	said	buy	bought
tell	told	put	put
read	read	bring	brought
write	wrote	meet	met
take	took	run	ran
have	had	sit	sat
see	saw	lose	lost
make	made	eat	ate
get	got	wear	wore
give	gave	know	knew
come	came	mean	meant
leave	left	let	let

These verbs are very frequent irregular verbs in conversational English.

5. At the end of the activity, count your money. How well do you know the irregular past tense verbs?

ACTIVITY **F** **1.** In groups of three or four, play a concentration game with irregular verbs. Each group should make 16 cards. Or use the cards on page 177. Eight cards should have the base form of an irregular verb. The other eight cards should have the simple past tense of each base form. Trade cards with another group.

2. Place the cards face down in a square with four cards going across and four cards going down. The first student should flip over two cards. If the two cards are the base form and the simple past tense form of the same verb, it is a match. If the cards don't make a match, the student should turn the cards back over. The other students each take turns trying to make a match. When a student makes a match, he or she keeps the cards. The goal of the game is to try to collect as many cards as possible.

Regular Verbs: Pronouncing *-ed* as /d/ and /t/

CD 3 Track 4

The *-ed* endings are very simple to pronounce. When we are going to say a regular past tense verb, we need to remember to do two things:

1. At the end of the verb, we need to add one more sound by moving our chin up and touching our tongue to the top (or roof) of the mouth behind our front teeth. By doing so, we will produce a /d/ or /t/.

ACTIVITY **G**

CD 3 Track 5

Listen to each verb. Listen for the final sound. Write in the box below if there is a final /d/ or /t/ sound.

Base Form	/d/ or /t/
try	
wash	
call	
place	
cough	
surprise	

Regular Verbs: Pronouncing *-ed* as /d/ and /t/

CD 3 Track 6

2. Besides touching our tongues to the roof of our mouth, there is one more thing we need to learn. The last sound of a verb can be of two kinds: *voiced* or *voiceless*.

Voiced sounds are when our vocal cords vibrate. For example, cover you ears with your hands. Now say, "Ah." You will hear your vocal cords vibrate. Now say, "Sh." Your vocal cords will not vibrate. "Ah" is a voiced sound; "sh" is a voiceless sound.

ACTIVITY **H**   Say each word below in the past tense and with your hands covering your ears.
Check ✔ if the **last** sound is voiced or voiceless.

Base Form	Voiced	Voiceless
try		
wash		
call		
place		
cough		
surprise		

Regular Verbs: Pronouncing *-ed* as /d/ and /t/

CD 3 Track 7

When we touch our tongue to the roof of our mouth to pronounce the *-ed* ending, we will produce the voiced sound /d/ if the last sound of the verb is voiced, and we will produce the voiceless sound /t/ if the last sound of the verb is voiceless. Look at the chart below.

Base Form	Voiced /d/	Voiceless /t/
try	tried	
wash		washed
call	called	
place		placed
cough		coughed
surprise	surprised	

 ACTIVITY **I**
CD 3 Track 8

1. Listen to each verb. If the verb is in the simple past tense form, stand up. If the verb is in the base form, sit down.

2. Listen again. Write the verb you hear next to the letter. For the verbs in the simple past tense, check ✔ if the final sound is /d/ or /t/.

Verb	/d/	/t/
a.		
b.		
c.		
d.		
e.		
f.		
g.		
h.		
i.		
j.		

LISTENING STRATEGIES AND PRONUNCIATION

Regular Verbs: Pronouncing -*ed* as /ɪd/

CD 3 Track 9

When a regular verb ends in a /d/ or /t/ sound (such as *need* or *visit*), our tongue is already on the roof of the mouth. In order to pronounce the -*ed* ending, we drop our chin and then move the chin up to touch the top of the mouth again saying, "/ɪd/."

Base Form	Simple Past	Pronunciation
count	counted	/countɪd/
treat	treated	/treatɪd/
start	started	/startɪd/
want	wanted	/wantɪd/
need	needed	/needɪd/
end	ended	/endɪd/

1. Listen to each verb. If the verb is in the simple past tense form, stand up. If the verb is in the base form, sit down.

2. Listen again. Write the verb you hear next to the letter. Then check ✔ if it's in the base form or in the simple past tense.

Verb	Base Form	Simple Past
a.		
b.		
c.		
d.		
e.		
f.		
g.		
h.		
i.		
j.		

Look at the chart of regular verbs below. Get out a mirror and place it in front of your mouth. As you listen, repeat the words and watch how your mouth moves. Make sure you touch your tongue to the top of your mouth behind your front teeth.

Base Form	Simple Past
wash	wash<u>ed</u>
start	start<u>ed</u>
stop	stopp<u>ed</u>
hug	hugg<u>ed</u>
watch	watch<u>ed</u>
call	call<u>ed</u>
attack	attack<u>ed</u>
chat	chatt<u>ed</u>
smile	smil<u>ed</u>
listen	listen<u>ed</u>

ACTIVITY **L** In pairs, sit facing each other. One student pronounces the base form or the simple past tense form of a verb from the chart on page 108. The other student says whether the verb is the base form or the simple past tense form. If a student hears a different form than what you said, make sure you are placing your tongue correctly.

ACTIVITY **M** Your instructor will say a base form of a verb, such as "stop," and then say the name of a student. That student will choose a past time expression below. Then the student will say a complete sentence with the verb in the simple past tense. For example: "I stopped at the mall yesterday." Here is another example: "decide." "Mary decided to go to Mexico two days ago."

last Monday	last week	last month	last year
three days ago	four days ago	five days ago	six days ago
yesterday	yesterday morning	yesterday afternoon	last night

GRAMMAR

Simple Past Tense: *Yes/No* Questions

Yes/no questions in the simple past tense are formed in the same way as *yes/no* questions in the simple present tense. There is only one difference—use *did* instead of *do* or *does* to show that the question is in the past tense.

Simple Present Tense Questions

| Do | you | eat out | once a week? |

Simple Past Tense Questions

| Did | you | eat out | once a week? |

ACTIVITY **N** Write *yes/no* questions about the sentence *I went shopping last night*.

a. Did you buy anything? _____

b. _____

c. _____

d. _____

e. _____

f. _____

 **ACTIVITY O**
CD 3 Track 12

1. Listen to students playing "20 Questions" with their instructor.

2. Play "20 Questions" with your instructor. Your class asks your instructor up to 20 *yes/no* questions about what he or she did on Saturday night. Your instructor can only respond with affirmative or negative answers. For example:

Useful
Expressions

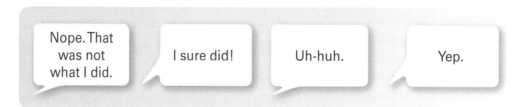

Nope. That was not what I did.

I sure did!

Uh-huh.

Yep.

GRAMMAR

Simple Past Tense: *Wh-* Questions

To form *wh-* questions in the simple past, insert a *wh-* word at the beginning of a *yes/no* question.

Where | did | you | go | last night?

ACTIVITY **P** Complete the conversation below with the correct *wh-* word.

A: Genine?

B: Yes?

A: May I talk to you for a second?

B: Sure.

A: I'm sorry I didn't come to your birthday party last night.

B: Oh, that's OK.

A: Well, I just want to explain . . .

B: Uh-huh.

A: My car got burglarized.

B: Oh, no! _____ was your car?
                    (a)

A: It was parked in front of my mom's house.

B: _____ did they do to the car?
          (b)

A: They broke the windows to steal a laptop.

B: Oh, no! _____ did you leave your laptop?
                    (c)

A: I left it on the back seat.

B: You should never leave stuff in your car. Put it in the trunk.

A: I know.

B: _____ did you do?
(d)

A: I called the police.

B: _____ did they say?
(e)

A: Well, they said there was not much they could do.

B: Oh, no.

A: They said I was lucky I didn't have my personal information on my laptop.

B: Thank goodness!

A: I know.

B: I'm sorry you had to go through all that. Are you all right?

A: Yeah, I'm OK.

ACTIVITY **Q**   Write *wh-* questions about the sentence below.

I went to the beach **last weekend.**

Remember to use the correct form for *wh-* questions in the simple past tense.

$$\downarrow$$

| Wh- | did | you | (verb) | last weekend? |

a. When did you go to the beach? _____

b. _____

c. _____

d. _____

e. _____

f. _____

g. _____

h. _____

i. _____

j. _____

ACTIVITY **R** Put the words in the correct order and write the sentences. Use correct punctuation.

| you | where | go | did |

a. _____

| you | spend | money | did | how much |

b. _____

| there | do | did | you | what |

c. _____

| how | go | you | did |

d. _____

| buy | why | did | that | you |

e. _____

| you | when | did | go | there |

f. _____

GRAMMAR

Simple Past Tense: Negative Statements

To form negative statements in the simple past tense, use *did not* (*didn't*) + the base form of the verb.

| I | did not | eat out | last night. |
| | didn't | | |

ACTIVITY **S** Write four sentences about things you *didn't* do last night.

a. *I didn't exercise.* _____

b. _____

c. _____

d. _____

e. _____

 ACTIVITY **T** Listen to each conversation. Near the end of the conversation, the narrator will
CD 3 Track 13   ask what you think the speaker did *not* do. Write your answer on the lines below
based on what you heard in the conversation. Then listen to the rest of the
conversation to check your answer.

Conversation 1: _____

Conversation 2: _____

Conversation 3: _____

ACTIVITY **U** **1.** One student will stand at the front of the classroom facing all the students,
with his or her back to the board. The instructor will write a sentence on the
board that shows a place that the instructor went to last weekend.

2. The other students in the class will make statements about what the instructor
did *not* do in that place. The student standing at the front of the classroom will
use these clues to guess where the instructor went.

 **3.** Listen to a group of students doing the same task.
CD 3 Track 14

Talking about Last Weekend

At the beginning of the week, it is common to ask people at work or school how their weekend was. Study the sequence of a typical conversation about one's weekend. Notice how it has a beginning, a middle, and an end.

A: Hi, there. How was your weekend? ⟶ **Greet the person.**
Ask about his or her weekend.

B: Great! ⟶ **Respond.**

A: What did you do? ⟶ **Ask a question.**

B: I went to a great restaurant with my family Saturday night. ⟶ **Talk about an event (what, who, where).**

A: Cool! What restaurant?

B: The Plaza at Plaza Bonita.

A: What kind of food do they serve there? ⟶ **React to the information.**
Ask more questions (past, present or future).

B: It's mainly American.

A: Is it expensive?

B: Not really.

A: I need to try it. ⟶ **Make a final comment.**

B: You'll love it! ⟶ **End the interaction.**

 ACTIVITY **V**
CD 3 Track 15

1. Listen as a student answers questions from her classmates about her weekend.

2. One student tells the class what he or she did on the weekend. The other students ask questions about the student's activity or activities.

 ACTIVITY **W**
CD 3 Track 16

1. Listen to a conversation about a student's weekend.

2. Work in pairs. You will simulate a conversation with another student. Follow the sequence below.

- Greet the person. Ask about his or her weekend.

- Respond.

- Ask a question.

- Talk about an event (who, what, where).

- React to the information. Ask more questions (past, present, future).
- Make a final comment.
- End the interaction.

3. Then repeat the activity with several different students.

Cultural Note	During a conversation, it is inappropriate to ask questions about money. A person's finances are considered personal information. Therefore, avoid asking questions related to money and finances, such as how much a person paid for something and how much a person earns.

REVIEW AND EXPAND

🔊 ACTIVITY **A**
CD 3 Track 17

1. Listen to a conversation about a student's weekend.

2. Write what you did last Saturday on the line below.

_____

3. As a class, stand in two lines facing each other. Ask and talk about each other's weekend. When the instructor claps his or her hands, the students in one line take a step to the right (the student at the beginning of that line then moves to the end) and repeat the activity. Continue until you return to your original partner. Use the expressions below.

Useful
Expressions

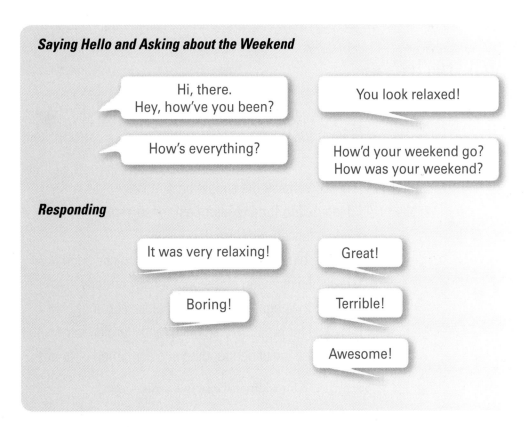

Saying Hello and Asking about the Weekend

Hi, there.
Hey, how've you been?

You look relaxed!

How's everything?

How'd your weekend go?
How was your weekend?

Responding

It was very relaxing!

Great!

Boring!

Terrible!

Awesome!

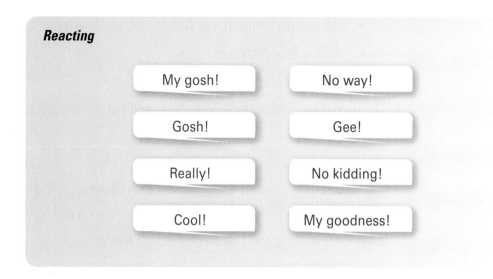

Reacting

My gosh!   No way!

Gosh!   Gee!

Really!   No kidding!

Cool!   My goodness!

ACTIVITY **B**   Your instructor will give each student a card similar to the one below*.
Get up and talk to six different people. Greet them and ask about the weekend.
Remember to react to the answers and make comments.

Example card:

> **INTERESTING!**
>
> **What/where:** went to the museum
> **When:** on Saturday
> **What happened:** saw an art exhibit and met the artist

EVALUATION

ACTIVITY **A**   Now that you have completed the activities in this chapter, complete the self-evaluation checklist below. Discuss your checklist with a classmate.

Self-Evaluation Checklist

- ☐ I used verbs in the simple past tense.
- ☐ I learned to form regular past tense verbs.
- ☐ I pronounced *-ed* correctly.
- ☐ I was able to identify voiceless and voiced sounds.
- ☐ I asked a question in the past tense correctly.
- ☐ I used the negative in the past tense correctly.
- ☐ I asked for repetition, spelling, and clarification when necessary.
- ☐ I checked my understanding and confirmed information when necessary.

*See page 178 for additional example cards.

ACTIVITY **B**   Look back at the chapter and the self-evaluation checklist above. What can you do this week to improve the skills you have learned in this chapter? Talk with a partner and write an action plan for how you can improve your skills this week.

Example   *I need to work on pronouncing the -ed endings of past tense verbs. I thought I was pronouncing it correctly, but I have realized that I don't pronounce it correctly for every verb. So, every time I use a regular verb in the past tense, I'm going to make sure I'm pronouncing the -ed ending correctly. If I realize I haven't, I'll go back in the conversation, say, "I mean," and pronounce the verb the correct way. I'll also practice general conversation on the weekend with my neighbor.*

Action Plan

GET STARTED

🔊 ACTIVITY **A**   Listen to three people explain what happened to them. Write each conversation
CD 3 Track 18   number below its corresponding picture.

a. _____

b. _____

c. _____

ACTIVITY **B**   **1.** Sometimes emergencies happen. Write on the lines below three reasons why
you might miss school or work.

a. <u>My mother is in the hospital.</u> _____

b. _____

c. _____

d. _____

2. Share your reasons with two other classmates.

LEARN AND PRACTICE

Simple Past Tense of *Be*: Statements with All Subject Pronouns

In Chapter 1, we studied the simple present of *be* (*am*, *is*, and *are*). In this chapter, we will study the simple past tense of *be* (*was* and *were*).

Simple Present of *Be*

| I | am | studious. |

| You | are | a good soccer player. |

| She He It | is | a student. |

| We You They | are | neighbors. |

Simple Past of *Be*

| I | was | studious. |

| You | were | a good soccer player. |

| She He It | was | a student. |

| We You They | were | neighbors. |

ACTIVITY **A**   Complete the conversations below with *was* or *were*.

CONVERSATION 1

A: How _____ your weekend?
(a)

B: Not bad. My dad and I rented some movies.

A: Cool!

B: Yeah. They _____ excellent!
(b)

A: What _____ they about?
(c)

B: They _____ all comedies.
(d)

A: Hi, there. You look tired.

B: Yeah. I _____ so busy this past weekend!
(e)

A: Why?

B: You know, midterm time.

A: Yeah. No kidding. Did you study a lot?

B: Yeah. And my husband _____ not home, so I had to cook.
(f)

A: Is he the cook at your house?

B: Oh, yeah. And a great one!

CONVERSATION 3

A: Mary, what happened? You look worried.

B: Gee, you don't know what happened to me today.

A: What?

B: I _____ coming to school when I saw a lost dog on the street.
(g)

A: Oh, no.

B: It _____ trying to cross the street.
(h)

A: Oh, my gosh!

B: It _____ a big dog!
(i)

A: What did you do?

B: I caught it and brought it home with me.

A: That's sweet.

B: I'm going to try to find the owner.

A: That's nice of you!

CONVERSATION 4

A: Hi, there.

B: Hi.

A: How was your weekend?

B: Great! I went on a brunch cruise with my family.

A: Really?

B: Yep. It _____ great! Everybody _____
(j)   (k)

really happy.

A: And hungry, I bet.

B: Oh, yeah! The boat _____ pretty big . . .
(l)

A: Uh-huh.

B: And the food _____ delicious.
(m)

A: Cool!

B: My grandparents _____ very happy to see all the family together.
(n)

A: I bet.

Simple Past Tense of *Be*: Questions with *You*

When you want to ask questions with *be*, invert the subject and the verb.

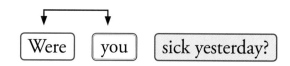

Were | you | sick yesterday?

ACTIVITY **B** Instructor Demo

1. Try to find out what kind of student your instructor was when he or she was in high school. Make a list of *Were you . . . ?* questions to ask your instructor. For example: *Were you on a sports team?*

2. Take turns asking your instructor questions. Find out as much as possible about what your instructor was like as a high school student.

ACTIVITY **C** Work in groups of four. Choose one student from the group to answer questions. The other three students should ask *Were you . . . ?* questions and find out as much as possible about what he or she was like as a high school student.

Simple Past Tense of *Be*: *Wh-* Questions

When you want to ask questions with a *wh-* word, place the *wh-* word at the beginning of the sentence.

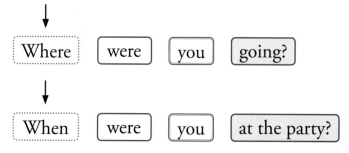

Where | were | you | going?

When | were | you | at the party?

ACTIVITY **D** First, read the conversation. Then complete the conversation below with
wh- questions and *be.* Use the simple past tense.

A mother is waiting for her teenage son to return home. It's 1:00 A.M. The door
opens. Mom is waiting on the couch.

A: _____?

B: Mom! You startled me! I was at José's house. I told you!

A: _____?

B: Mom, I told you. Anthony, Ali, Sue, Manuel, and I were there.

A: _____ José's parents there?

B: Yes. They _____ there.

A: _____?

B: What girl?

A: The girl that dropped you off.

B: That _____ José's mom!

A: Oh!

GRAMMAR

Simple Past Tense of *Be*: Negative Statements with *I*

To make a negative statement, insert *not* after *be.*

| I | was | not | home when you called. |

You can contract *be* and *not.*

| I | wasn't | home when you called. |

ACTIVITY **E** Write on the lines below four things you were *not* when you were in high school.

a. I was not tall. _____

b. _____

c. _____

d. _____

e. _____

ACTIVITY **F**
CD 3 Track 19

1. Listen to a group of students talking about what they were like in high school. The students are answering questions in the simple past tense with *be* and other verbs.

2. Choose one student to answer the group's questions. Find out as much as possible about that student when he or she was in high school.

SPEAKING STRATEGIES

Hesitating

When we speak, we need to gain time to think while we construct what to say. One of these strategies is called *hesitating*. We can hesitate while speaking by:

- pausing (briefly stop speaking and then begin again),
- saying *uh* or *um,*
- or repeating a word. (For example: *I, I am happy to see you.*)

ACTIVITY **G**
CD 3 Track 20

Listen to the conversation. The speakers use different hesitating strategies as they speak. Write options from the box below on the lines in the conversation.

(pause)	*uh*	*um*	(repeat)

CONVERSATION

A: Hey, how are you?

B: Fine.

A: You didn't come last class. I was worried.

B: Oh, I _____, _____, I couldn't come
     (a)   (b)

because I _____ overslept.
          (c)

A: You what?

B: Yeah, it was my birthday the night before . . .

A: Oh, I see.

B: So, I _____, _____ *kinda* went to bed
     (d)   (e)

too late.

A: OK. I'm glad you weren't sick.

B: Nope. I'm fine.

A: Good.

1. Listen to a group of students answering questions about their weekend.

2. Your instructor will ask the students questions about their weekend. When it is your turn, remember to use the speaking strategies you have learned. Hesitate as you speak to help you construct the language. Make sure your verbs are in the past tense.

GRAMMAR

Using Connectors: *So, And,* and *'Cause*

When we talk, we use words to connect thoughts together. These connectors are not always the same for speaking and writing. Look at the examples of these words used in writing and in speaking.

Writing	Speaking
I'd like to let you know why you haven't heard from me. I just moved out of my old apartment **because** the rent is too expensive for me. I was very busy last week. I moved out on Monday, **and** I had to find another roommate, too. I don't have a phone at home yet, so please call me on my cell. Talk to you later.	Lorena, this is Eli . . . um . . . I didn't call you last week **'cause** I um had to move out of my apartment, . . . **and** I . . . um . . . had only two days **'cause** my rent went up so much . . . it was terrible . . . **and** I had to find another roommate too **'cause** Ann didn't want to leave the apartment. . . **So,** um . . . can you give me a call whenever you can? Please call my cell though **'cause** I don't have a landline yet. Bye.

In writing, you can use *so, and,* and *'cause* as connectors only once within a sentence. In speaking, *so, and,* and *'cause* are frequently used, and they are used repeatedly to connect thoughts.

Look at the how the connectors are used to link thoughts from the conversation.

Problem
I didn't call you last week   **'cause** ⟶

Explanation
I had to move out of my apartment.

↓

so

Favor
Can you give me a call whenever you can?

Complete the conversation below with *so, and,* or *'cause*. Then listen to the conversations and check your answers.

CONVERSATION 1

A: Mr. Abdul?

B: Yes?

A: May I speak with you?

B: Sure.

A: I, uh . . . didn't bring my homework today . . .

B: Uh-huh.

A: _____ I worked on the weekend. . . .
(a)

B: Um.

A: _____ I had to do some stuff for my mom.
(b)

B: OK.

A: _____, I didn't have time.
(c)

B: OK.

A: _____, I was wondering . . .
(d)

B: Yes?

A: May I bring it tomorrow?

B: Since you're a good student . . .

A: Thanks.

B: That's OK.

A: Thanks a lot, Mr. Abdul. I appreciate it.

CONVERSATION 2

A: Dr. Boyoke?

B: Yes?

A: Do you have a minute?

B: Sure. How can I help you?

A: Dr. Boyoke, I left early yesterday . . .

B: I noticed that . . .

A: _____ I got a call from my husband . . .
(e)

B: Uh-huh.

A: _____ our car got stolen.
(f)

B: Oh, no! I'm sorry to hear that!

A: Thanks. I just wanted you to know why I left early.

B: That's quite all right. Don't worry. I hope you find your car.

A: Thanks.

ACTIVITY **J** 1. Write on the lines below a problem, an explanation, and a favor you want to ask your instructor.

Problem

_____

_____

Explanation

_____

_____

Favor

_____

_____

2. Read the conversation introductions. Then add two more ways you can introduce the conversation.

Introduction

May I come in?

Do you have a minute?

Can I speak with you?

_____

_____

3. Write two ways for you to thank your instructor.

Saying "Thanks"

Thank you.

Thanks anyway. (if the answer is *no*)

Thanks. I appreciate it.

_____

_____

4. Use the problem from Step 1 and have a conversation with your instructor. Do not look at your paper. Your instructor will react. Hesitate to give yourself time to think.

Explaining Past Problems

Sometimes you have emergencies or problems that prevent you from completing a task. It's important to be able to explain to your boss or instructor what happened. You have to *introduce* the story, tell the *problem,* and *explain* what happened. You can ask for a *favor,* but you don't have to. You should always end the conversation by *thanking* the person for listening.

Introduction	→	**A:** Good morning, Dr. Levine. May I come in?
		B: Oh, sure. Come on in.
Problem	→	**A:** Thanks.
		B: Uh-huh
		A: I, um, I didn't come to class on Friday . . .
		B: Uh-huh
Explanation	→	**A:** 'Cause my car broke down on the highway on my way to school.
		B: Oh, no. That sounds terrible!
Favor (Optional)	→	**A:** So, I was wondering . . .
		B: Uh-huh?
		A: Can I take the test in class today?
		B: Yes, sure.
Thanks	→	**A:** Thanks a lot.
		B: No problem. I'm glad you're not hurt.
		A: Thanks.

ACTIVITY **K** Work in pairs. Student A will play the instructor. Student B will play himself or herself. Student B will explain a problem to Student A. Follow the sequence of the conversation above and use *so, and,* and *'cause.* Then, Student B should create a conversation with two additional Student As.

Listening for Stressed Words

In Chapter 6, we learned how to use some reduced words (reductions). In English, we reduce certain words in a sentence, and we stress the most important words (content words) in the same sentence. When we stress words, we make them longer and louder. Stress and reductions contribute to the rhythm of English.

🔊 **ACTIVITY L**
CD 3 Track 23

Listen to the conversation from Activity A again. Write the stressed words on the lines below. You can hear them clearly because they are longer and louder.

CONVERSATION 1

A: _____, Dr. Jeffrey. May I come in?
(a)

B: Oh, oh, _____. Come on in.
(b)

A: Thanks.

B: So, how can I help you?

A: Oh, I, um . . . I'm here _____. . . .
(c)

B: Uh-huh.

A: I, um, I _____ to class on _____ . . .
(d) (e)

B: Uh-huh.

A: 'Cause I _____ a _____ on my way to _____.
(f) (g) (h)

B: Oh, no. That's _____! Are you _____?
(i) (j)

A: Oh yeah . . . I'm _____ now, but, uh . . . I had to go to the
(k)

_____ room.
(l)

B: Oh, no . . . I'm sorry to hear that.

A: Yeah. It was scary . . . but, uh, the problem is that I . . . I didn't

_____ the _____.
(m) (n)

B: Oh. The test on Monday.

A: Uh-huh. So, um . . . I know you _____ give make up tests . . .
(o)

B: Well, . . . usually I don't . . . but this is different . . . it was an

_____ though.
(p)

A: Exactly. I have the _____ from the ER. . . . Here.
(q)

B: Good. Can I make a copy?

A: Sure. So, . . . I was wondering . . .

B: Uh?

A: Can I _____ the test _____ today?
(r)   (s)

B: Yes, sure.

A: Thanks a lot.

B: No problem. I'm glad you're not hurt.

A: Thanks a lot.

Cultural Note In an American college, it is very important to contact your instructor when you have a problem. Office hours are hours that instructors set aside to talk to students. You usually don't need to make an appointment if you are going to stop by your instructor's office during office hours. If you can't stop by during office hours, you should make an appointment by e-mail, phone, or in person before or after class.

REVIEW: PRONUNCIATION

Simple Past Tense: Pronouncing *-ed* in Regular Verbs

CD 3 Track 24

In Chapter 7, you learned how to form the simple past tense form of regular verbs by adding *-ed*. The *-ed* ending can have three different sounds: /d/, /t/, or /ɪd/.

ACTIVITY **M** 1. Work with a partner. Student A should say each word aloud to Student B. Student B should listen for the verb and check ✔ the sound they hear. Remember that the *-ed* ending can have three different sounds: **/d/**, **/t/**, or **/ɪd/**.

2. Switch roles. Student B will say each word aloud and Student A will check the sound they hear.

Verbs	/d/	/t/	/ɪd/	Verbs	/d/	/t/	/ɪd/
danced				studied			
waited				played			
worked				needed			
washed				stuffed			
watched				corrected			

CD 3 Track 25

3. Listen and check your answers. Compare your answers with your partner's.

REVIEW AND EXPAND

ACTIVITY Work in groups of three. Each group needs dice. Each student will need a different coin to use as a marker. Place the coins on the **START LINE**. Decide who goes first, second, and so on. Student 1 rolls the dice and moves his or her coin. Student 1 reads the instructions and does what is asked. The other students take turns until someone reaches the finish line. Use the expressions below.

Your friend has been waiting for you at the movie theater for 15 minutes. Call him or her, explain why, and apologize.	Go back 1 space.	Tell your classmates an unusual story that happened to you last night. Start with "You'll never guess what happened to me last night."	Find out as much as possible about what your classmates did last night.

Go back 3 spaces.

You missed your test last class. Explain to your instructor what happened.

Lose a turn.

You were 15 minutes late to class. Explain to your instructor why you were late.

START LINE

Lose a turn.

Find out what your classmates did last summer.

Find out something you did last weekend that your classmates didn't do.

You told one of your classmates you were going to call over the weekend, but you didn't. Explain to him or her what happened and apologize.

FINISH

Useful Expressions

It's your turn.

Now, it's my turn.

Hurry. Roll the dice.

You are here, not here.

ACTIVITY **B**   Work with a partner. You and a partner will choose one relationship below. Create a dialog. Then present your dialog to the class. The other students have to guess the relationship that exists between you and your partner.

Relationship 1 two good friends	**Relationship 2** a student and an instructor	**Relationship 3** an employee and a boss	**Relationship 4** two classmates

EVALUATION

ACTIVITY **A**   Now that you have completed the activities in this chapter, complete the self-evaluation checklist below. Discuss your checklist with a classmate.

Self-Evaluation Checklist

☐ I used the simple past tense correctly.

☐ I explained a problem using verbs in the past tense.

☐ I hesitated to give myself time to construct what I wanted to say.

☐ I connected my thoughts with *so, and*, and *'cause*.

☐ I asked a favor politely and said "thank you."

☐ I listened for and identified stressed words in a sentence.

☐ I pronounced *-ed* endings correctly.

☐ I asked for repetition, spelling, and clarification when necessary.

☐ I checked and confirmed information when necessary.

ACTIVITY **B**   Look back at the chapter and the self-evaluation checklist above. What can you do this week to improve the skills you have learned in this chapter? Talk with a partner and write an action plan for how you can improve your skills this week.

Example   When I explain problems, I sometimes forget to use the verb in the past tense. I need to make sure I use the past tense and that I pronounce the -ed sound correctly. So, every day for about ten minutes, I'll practice a conversation where I explain a problem and ask for a favor. I will make sure that I'm using the past tense when I need to.

Action Plan

9 | Would You Like to Go?

GET STARTED

🔊 ACTIVITY **A**
CD 3 Track 26

Listen to three people inviting others to do something. Write on the lines below what they are inviting them to do.

Conversation 1: _____

Conversation 2: _____

Conversation 3: _____

ACTIVITY **B** **1.** On the lines below, write four things you like to do on the weekend.

a. I like to go shopping on the weekend. _____

b. _____

c. _____

d. _____

e. _____

2. Look at the sentences from Activity B. Who do you like to do these activities with? Write four sentences below.

a. <u>I like to go shopping with my best friend</u>

b. _____

c. _____

d. _____

e. _____

 ACTIVITY **C**
CD 3 Track 27

1. Listen to a group of students talk about their favorite weekend activities.

2. Work with a partner. Talk to your partner about your favorite weekend activities and who you like to do these things with.

Useful
Expressions

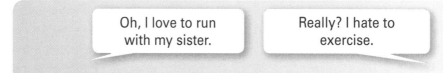

Oh, I love to run with my sister.

Really? I hate to exercise.

LEARN AND PRACTICE

GRAMMAR

Inviting with *Would* and *Want*

When we want to invite someone to do something with us, we need to ask politely. Look at the part of a question below:

| go | | shopping on the weekend? |

Now, in front of it, add *Would you like to*.

| Would you like to | ⟶ | go | | shopping on the weekend? |

You can also add *Do you want to*.

| Do you want to | ⟶ | go | | shopping on the weekend? |

Responding to Invitations

When someone invites you to do something, you can accept the invitation or turn it down. When you turn down an invitation, you need to be very polite. You should apologize and give an explanation. Remember that when you turn down an invitation and give an explanation, you can talk about things you have to do (obligation), things you want to do (desire), and things you are unable to do (inability).

Accepting an Invitation	Turning Down an Invitation
Sure. I'd love to.	I'm so sorry, but . . .
That's a great idea!	Sorry, I really can't. I . . .
It sounds fantastic!	Oh, I'd love to, but . . .

Cultural Note In American culture, it is important to avoid using the word *no* when turning down an invitation. Saying *no* may sound rude. To politely turn down an invitation, say *sorry* instead and explain why you cannot accept.

ACTIVITY A Imagine someone is inviting you to see a movie on the weekend. Write two responses accepting the invitation and two responses turning it down.

a. _____

b. _____

c. _____

d. _____

Listen to two conversations. For each conversation, decide whether the response is **polite** or **impolite**. Circle the correct answer. Discuss with a partner why you chose that answer.

Conversation 1: polite   impolite

Conversation 2: polite   impolite

ACTIVITY **C** Work in groups of four. Choose one student to be the secretary. (The secretary is the only one who can record your group's answers.) At the start of each round, your instructor will invite you to do something. Your group will have two minutes to turn the invitation down by writing polite excuses. The secretary will write down the group's answers.

Round 1: Pretend your instructor is a classmate. He or she will invite you to do something. Write down as many explanations expressing **obligation** as possible.

For example:

> **Invitation:** Would you like to have lunch with me in the cafeteria after class?

List of excuses expressing obligation:

> Sorry, but I need to pick up my son at school.
>
> Sorry, I've got to study for a test I have at 1:00.
>
> I'd love to, but I have to leave right after class today.

Round 2: Pretend your instructor is a friend. He or she will invite you to do something. Write down as many explanations expressing **desire** as you can.

For example:

> **Invitation:** Would you like to go see a movie with me and some friends Friday after class?

List of excuses expressing desire:

> Sorry, but I want to leave early on Friday so I can miss the traffic.
>
> I really can't. I want to relax after class. I've had a very stressful week.

Round 3: Pretend your instructor is a classmate. He or she will invite you to do something. Write down as many explanations expressing both **obligation** and **desire** as you can.

 ACTIVITY **D**
CD 3 Track 29

1. Listen to the conversation. The student is turning down an invitation.

2. Half of the students will write down an invitation. The other half of the students will stand along the walls of the classroom. The students with an invitation will go around inviting others to do something with them. The other students can't accept. They must give an excuse using obligation or desire. (Remember to be polite when turning down the invitation!)

REVIEW: GRAMMAR

Responding to an Invitation Using the Present, Past, and Future Tenses

When we turn down an invitation, it is always polite to give an explanation. This explanation can be in the present, past, or future tense.

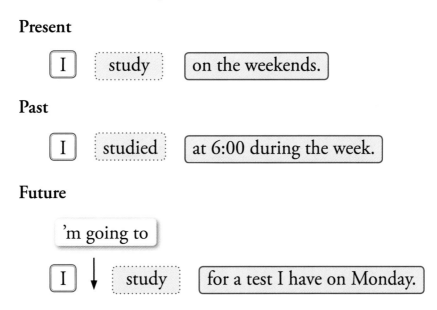

Present

I | study | on the weekends.

Past

I | studied | at 6:00 during the week.

Future

'm going to

I ↓ study | for a test I have on Monday.

ACTIVITY **E**   Read each sentence. Identify if the underlined portion is in the present, past, or future tense.

CONVERSATION 1

A: Hi, there. What <u>are you doing</u>? _____
(a)

B: Nothing important. Why?

A: Well, I was wondering . . .

B: Huh?

A: Would you like to get some coffee?

B: Now?

A: Uh-huh.

B: Well, there is a tiny problem though.

A: What's that?

B: <u>I'm going to leave in about 15 minutes.</u> _____
(b)

A: Oh.

B: <u>I'm going to meet a friend at the gym today.</u> _____
(c)

A: Oh, well, we can have coffee another time.

B: OK, then.

CONVERSATION 2

A: What's up?

B: Hi.

A: I was looking for you.

B: Oh?

A: Would you like to have lunch with me after class on Friday?

B: On Friday?

A: Uh-huh.

B: Well, um . . . <u>after class on Fridays I always go straight home</u>. I have

lunch with a friend. _____
(d)

A: Oh, I see. How about Thursday instead of Friday?

B: Um . . . I . . . I'm not sure. . . . The problem is that <u>I don't come to school</u>

<u>on Thursdays until 4:00 P.M.</u> _____
(e)

A: Oh.

B: Yeah.

A: Well, um . . . I guess I need to figure out something else then.

B: Yeah.

A: How about coffee right now?

B: Sounds good.

CONVERSATION 3

A: How was dinner last night?

B: Great!

A: Cool!

B: <u>The food was great, the date was great. We had a great time!</u>

_____
(f)

A: Fantastic!

B: Yeah, in fact, I was wondering . . . would you like to eat Brazilian barbecue with me next weekend?

A: Oh, I'd love to, but I, um . . . just went to a Brazilian <u>restaurant last</u>

<u>weekend.</u> _____
(g)

B: Oh, I see.

A: Yeah. It's a lot of meat, so . . .

B: Yeah, I understand.

ACTIVITY **F**   Work in groups of four. Choose one student to be the secretary. (The secretary is the only one who can record your group's answers.) At the start of each round, your instructor will ask for a favor. Your group will have two minutes to turn the favor down by writing polite excuses. The secretary will write down the group's answers.

Round 1: Pretend your instructor is a classmate. He or she will ask you for a favor. Write down as many explanations as you can. Use the **present tense** for all of your excuses.

For example:

> **Favor:** Can I borrow your notebook for the weekend?

List of excuses in the present tense:

> Sorry, but I study **on the weekends**.
>
> Sorry, **on Saturdays** I meet with the tutor.
>
> I'd love to, but **on Sundays** I study composition.
>
> I'm sorry. I really can't. Two other classmates and I study together **on Sundays**.

Round 2: Pretend your instructor is a neighbor. He or she will ask you for a favor. Write down as many explanations as you can. Use the **past tense** for all of your excuses. Think about something that has happened to you that makes it impossible for you to do the favor.

For example:

> **Favor:** Can you help me move on Saturday?

List of excuses in the past tense:

> Sorry, but I **hurt** my hand at the gym **yesterday** and I can't lift anything.
>
> Sorry, I'd love to, but my mom **invited** me to go shopping with her and I **accepted**.
>
> I really can't. I just **bought** a ticket to go to Cancún on Saturday.
>
> I'm sorry. I **promised** my son to take him to the beach.

Round 3: Pretend your instructor is a coworker. He or she will ask you for a favor. Write down as many explanations in the **future tense** as you can.

For example:

> **Favor:** Can you help me move on Saturday?

List of excuses in the future tense:

> Sorry, but on Saturday I'**m going to** take a very long test.
>
> Sorry, this coming Saturday my family and I **are going to** spend the weekend out of town.
>
> I'd love to, but on Saturday I'**m going to** study for a very important test I have on Monday.
>
> I really can't. On Saturday my sister **is going to** fly in to town. I need to pick her up at the airport.

 ACTIVITY **G** **1.** Listen to a student asking a favor of a classmate.

CD 3 Track 30

2. Half of the students will write down a favor. The other half of the students will stand around the walls facing the inside of the classroom. The students with the favors will go around asking others to help them. The other students must give an excuse using the present, past, or future tense. (Remember to be polite when saying you can't do a favor!)

Intonation for Invitiations

 In Chapter 4, we studied rising and falling intonation. It's important to remember that rising intonation is when we raise our voice at the end of a thought. Falling intonation is when we lower it at the end of a thought.

CD 3 Track 31

With a *yes/no* question, we use rising intonation.

For example:

Would you like to go shopping this afternoon? (↑)

When we answer it, we use falling intonation.

For example:

Sorry. I've got to study for a test I have tomorrow. (↓)

 ACTIVITY **H** **1.** Listen to the sentences and circle if the person is inviting or responding to the invitation.

CD 3 Track 31

    a. inviting   responding to the invitation

    b. inviting   responding to the invitation

    c. inviting   responding to the invitation

    d. inviting   responding to the invitation

    e. inviting   responding to the invitation

2. Work in pairs. Write down two invitations on the lines below. Invite your partner to do these things. Move your fingers up when you are inviting. When your partner invites you to do something, move your fingers down as you respond.

_____

_____

Chapter 9 | Would You Like to Go?   145

Speaking and Writing Are Different

This semester, you have learned a lot of things about speaking. Let's review some of these strategies.

Remember that the way you write is different from the way you speak. When you talk, you use expressions, hesitate, repeat words, and use strategies that are specific for conversation.

ACTIVITY **1** Read the two interactions below. Then discuss and answer the questions with your classmates.

Interaction 1	Interaction 2
A: How's it going? B: OK. A: Wanna do something? B: Not really. A: Huh? B: Just wanna stay home and relax. A: OK, then. Let's do that. Wanna watch a movie? B: Sure. What movie? A: *Lord of the Rings*? B: OK. A: All right, then.	Sweetheart, I had to leave early today, but I'd like to know what you want to do tonight. Maybe we can watch *Lord of the Rings* together. Give me a call on my cell. Me XOXO

a. Which interaction is a letter and which one is a conversation? How do you know?

b. Tell your class the characteristics of spoken language that you found in the conversation.

c. Is this conversation formal or informal? How do you know?

d. Who are the people involved in this conversation? How do you know?

Identifying Speaking Strategies

When you speak, you use a variety of strategies. Some of the strategies you have learned in this book are hesitating, connecting thoughts, talking around a word, starting and ending interactions politely, being more or less formal, and being polite or impolite.

ACTIVITY **J** Find examples of the speaking strategies from the box in the conversation below. Put the number of the speaking strategy over the place where it appears.

A: Hey, Judith.

B: Hi.

A: I need a favor.

B: Sure.

A: Well, I, um . . . I . . . promised to bake a cake . . . for my wife.

B: Oh, that's sweet.

A: So, I, um . . . the . . . but my mixer is not working.

B: Oh.

A: So, I was wondering, can I borrow yours?

B: Um . . . my, um . . . sister has my mixer. I'm sorry.

A: Oh. That's OK.

B: Well, you can borrow my, um . . . what do you call that thingy we use for beating eggs?

A: Oh, you mean *whisk*?

B: Yeah. I have one. Wanna borrow it?

A: Oh, no thanks. I, um . . . I, I'm going . . . I need a mixer.

B: Sorry.

A: Oh. That's all right. Thanks anyway.

> **Speaking Strategies**
> 1. Hesitating
> 2. Connecting Thoughts
> 3. Talking around a Word
> 4. Starting and Ending Interactions Politely
> 5. Being More or Less Formal
> 6. Being Polite or Impolite

Negotiating Strategies

When you speak, you interact with other people. The way you say things is as important as what you say. The negotiating strategies that you have learned this semester include asking for repetition, asking for clarification, checking understanding, and confirming understanding.

ACTIVITY **K** Find examples of the negotiating strategies from the box in the conversation below. Put the number of the negotiating strategy over the place where it appears.

A: Next. How can I help you?

B: I'd like to deposit this check in my account . . .

A: Checking account?

B: That's correct.

B: And . . . also . . . get some money out.

A: OK. Can I have your account number, please?

Negotiation Strategies
1. Asking for Repetition
2. Asking for Clarification
3. Checking Understanding
4. Confirming Understanding

B: Oh, sure. 33056789.

A: Did you say eighty-nine or ninety-eight?

B: Eighty-nine.

A: Oh, OK. Can I see your photo ID?

B: Oh, sure.

A: Thanks.

A few seconds later . . .

A: Here is your receipt.

B: Thanks.

A: How much cash do you want out?

B: Fifty.

A: Five-oh.

B: Correct.

A: Oh, fifty. OK. And here it is. Anything else?

B: No, thanks. That's all.

A: Have a good day.

B: You, too.

Listening for the Main Ideas and Listening for Details

You have learned that you use different strategies when you listen for the main ideas and when you listen for details. Let's review these listening strategies.

The **main idea** of an interaction are related to what happened, where, who, why, etc. They are things that you can picture in your minds while people talk to you. You usually keep a mental picture of these things.

Details are pieces of information you need to write down or you may forget them, such as addresses, telephone numbers, and birthdays.

ACTIVITY **L**   What are the main ideas? What are details? Look at the sentences below. Circle **MI** if the item requires that you listen for the main idea. Circle **D** if the item requires that you listen for a detail.

a. The people in the interaction are friends.	**MI**	**D**
b. Both live close to the campus.	**MI**	**D**
c. Larry lives on Oak Street.	**MI**	**D**
d. They are both good students.	**MI**	**D**
e. They don't like to drive.	**MI**	**D**
f. John's cell phone number is 878-5634.	**MI**	**D**

ACTIVITY **M**   Now listen to the conversation. Circle *T* if the statement is true. Circle *F* if the statement is false. Correct the false statements.

CD 3 Track 32

a. The people in the interaction are friends.	T	F
b. Both live close to the campus.	T	F
c. Larry lives on Oak Street.	T	F
d. They are both good students.	T	F
e. Larry doesn't like to drive.	T	F
f. John's cell phone number is 878-5634.	T	F

REVIEW AND EXPAND

ACTIVITY **A** **1.** You are going to practice offering, accepting, and turning down an invitation. Form two circles with an equal number of students in each one—an outside circle and an inside circle. Each student in the outside circle must stand facing a student in the inside circle. The students in the inside circle will be called Group A, and the students on the outside circle will be called students Group B.

2. Each student in Group A will invite a student from Group B to do something with him or her. Students should use the schedules below and discuss a date and time. Student can either accept or turn down the invitation. Every time the instructor claps his or her hands, the students in Group B should move to the right around the circle until they return to their original partners.

Group A

Monday	Tuesday	Wednesday	Thursday	Friday	Saturday	Sunday
Lunch at 1:00 with Leslie	Class from 8:00 to 1:00	Free	Gym at 9:00 P.M.	Class from 9:00 to 12:00 Gym at 3:00	Clean the house	Free

Group B

Monday	Tuesday	Wednesday	Thursday	Friday	Saturday	Sunday
Dinner at 7:00 with a friend	Class from 8:00 to 1:00 Free afternoon	Class from 2:00 to 4:00	Meeting at 11:00	Gym from 9:00 to 12:00	Free	Free

ACTIVITY **B** **1.** The class will be divided into two groups of students: Group A and Group B.

Group A: Students in Group A should each think about a favor or an invitation. Each student in this group should complete the chart below.

Favors	Invitations
A favor you would ask a neighbor: _____ _____ _____	An invitation you would make to a classmate: _____ _____ _____
A favor you would ask your instructor: _____ _____ _____	An invitation you would make to your parents: _____ _____ _____

Group B: Choose if you want to be a **neighbor, classmate, instructor**, or **parent**. Take a sheet of paper from your notebook and write **neighbor, classmate, instructor**, or **parent** on it. Display it on your desk. The students in the classroom need to know who you are.

CD 3 Track 33

2. Group A will walk around the classroom asking Group B members for favors or making invitations. Before you begin, listen to two students doing the same task. Use the phrases below to help you.

Past	Present	Future
Yesterday, I . . . On my last birthday, I . . .	On Mondays, I . . . . Every Friday afternoon, I . . .	Tomorrow, I'm going to . . . After class, I'm going to . . .

Obligation	Desire
I have to . . . I need to . . . I've got to . . .	I want to . . . I'd like to . . .

EVALUATION

ACTIVITY **A** Now that you have completed the activities in this chapter, complete the self-evaluation checklist below. Discuss your checklist with a classmate.

Self-Evaluation
Checklist

☐ I made invitations using *would* or *want*.

☐ I asked for a favor politely.

I used the following in my invitations (Circle all that apply):

Past   Present   Future   Inability   Desire   Obligation

☐ I started and ended interactions appropriately.

☐ I was able to listen for main ideas and details.

☐ I said "no" politely.

☐ I gave an excuse when I said "no."

☐ I connected my thoughts with *so*, *then*, *and*, and *'cause*.

☐ I hesitated to help construct my thoughts.

☐ I asked for repetition, spelling, and clarification when necessary.

☐ I checked and confirmed information when necessary.

☐ I was able to be more or less formal, depending on the situation.

ACTIVITY **B** Look back at the chapter and the self-evaluation checklist above. What can you do this week to improve the skills you have learned in this chapter? Talk with a partner and write an action plan for how you can improve your skills this week.

Example   I have noticed that I use the present and future tenses often, but I usually forget to use the past tense. Also, I don't know the past tense of many irregular verbs. So, I have decided to study the irregular past every day and make cards so I can memorize the forms. Also, when I talk, I'm going to pay attention to whether I am using the past tense. I'll focus on the past tense during my conversation group, too.

Action Plan

10 | I'd Like to Make an Appointment

GET STARTED

 ACTIVITY **A**   Listen to three people making appointments. Write on the lines below where they
CD 3 Track 34   are going.

1. _____   **2.** _____

3. _____

ACTIVITY **B**   With a partner, make a list of places you have to make appointments before visiting

a. *doctor's office* _____

b. _____

c. _____

LEARN AND PRACTICE

REVIEW: LISTENING STRATEGIES

Listening for Details

In Chapter 4, you were introduced to listening for details. Remember that details
are specific pieces of information—things we need to write down or we will
forget. Addresses, telephone numbers, and birthdays are examples of details.

ACTIVITY A Listen to the conversations again. Answer the qestions about each conversation.

CD 3 Track 35

CONVERSATION 1

a. What's the patient's name? _____

b. What time and day is the appointment? _____

CONVERSATION 2

c. What's the student's name? _____

d. What's the student's ID number? _____

e. What time and day is the appointment? _____

CONVERSATION 3

f. What's the student's name? _____

g. What class is she talking about and what time is the class? _____

h. What time and day is the appointment? _____

GRAMMAR

Making Appointments

When you need to set a time and day to see a professional, you need to make an appointment. You often make appointments to see doctors, dentists, and counselors. You can use *I'd like to . . .* when you want to make appointments.

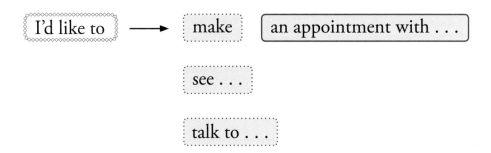

ACTIVITY **B** In pairs, discuss where you would say each of the sentences below.

- **I'd like to** make an appointment for a driving test.
- **I'd like to** make an appointment with my counselor.
- **I'd like to** see the dean.
- **I'd like to** talk to Dr. Boyoke.

You are trying to make an appointment at each of the following locations. Write a sentence in the lines below. Follow the example from the box on page 154.

(at school) _____

(at work) _____

(at the dentist) _____

Cultural Note When you say you want to make an appointment, the assistant that is talking to you usually asks some questions in order to find the best time and day for you.

🔊 ACTIVITY **D**
CD 3 Track 36
Listen to the conversations again. In the right column, write the number of the conversation in which you hear each question.

Questions	Conversation
a. Mornings or afternoons?	
b. What's your name?	
c. Can I have your name and student ID number?	
d. How about tomorrow after class?	
e. Can you get here 15 minutes before the appointment?	
f. Well, how about Friday? Around 9:00?	
g. Are you a new patient?	
h. Can you spell your last name?	

ACTIVITY **E** **1.** Your teacher will put blank sheets of paper on the wall around the classroom. With a partner, stand in front of one of the sheets of paper. Choose where you work.

dentist's office   admissions   dean's office   doctor's office   lawyer's office

2. With your partner, write on the sheet of paper the questions you would ask people calling to make an appointment.

3. When you have finished, move to the next sheet of paper. Read the questions. Where do these students work? Look at two other sheets of paper and try to figure out where the other students work.

Interactions Have a Beginning, a Middle, and an End

It is very important to know how to start and end an interaction politely so you can give a good impression. Many times, even in brief interactions, there is a beginning, a middle, and an end to the conversation. This is considered friendly and polite. Using correct grammar is very important, but being polite and appropriate is as important as using correct grammar.

ACTIVITY **F** Identify the parts of the conversation below. Then write in each set of parentheses the letter that corresponds to that part of the conversation.

---

a. Thanking and saying good-bye

b. Saying why you are calling

c. Asking for personal information

d. Repeating the time and day of the appointment

e. Negotiating time and day

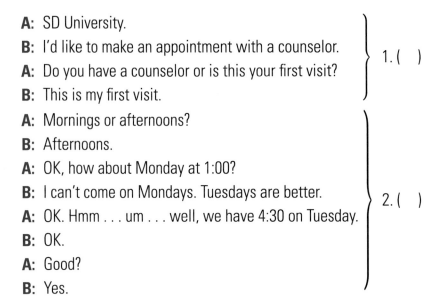

A: SD University.
B: I'd like to make an appointment with a counselor.
A: Do you have a counselor or is this your first visit?
B: This is my first visit.
} 1. ( )

A: Mornings or afternoons?
B: Afternoons.
A: OK, how about Monday at 1:00?
B: I can't come on Mondays. Tuesdays are better.
A: OK. Hmm . . . um . . . well, we have 4:30 on Tuesday.
B: OK.
A: Good?
B: Yes.
} 2. ( )

A: Can I have your name and student ID number?

B: Sure. Christina Borges.

A: Can you spell your last name?

B: Sure. It's B-O-R-G-E-S.

A: *G* as in *good*?

B: Yes. My ID number is 768950.

3. ( )

A: OK. We'll see you on Tuesday at 4:30.

4. ( )

B: Thanks.

A: No problem.

5. ( )

CD 3 Track 37 ◀)) ACTIVITY **G**   Instructor Demo

1. Listen to the conversation. A patient is calling Dr. Soto's office to make an appointment for next week.

2. Your instructor will be Dr. Soto's assistant. You are the patient calling for an appointment for next week. Your instructor will answer the phone. You will look at My Schedule below. Your instructor will look at Dr. Soto's Schedule on the next page.

3. Repeat the task with a classmate.

My Schedule

	Monday	Tuesday	Wednesday	Thursday	Friday
9:00	meeting w/boss	work			work
10:00		work		meeting w/boss	work
11:00		work			
12:00	meeting w/boss	lunch		class	
1:00					dentist
2:00					
3:00			pick up mother at airport		
4:00					
5:00					

Doctor Soto's Schedule

	Monday	Tuesday	Wednesday	Thursday	Friday
9:00		meeting w/ director	meeting w/ assistants		
10:00	Bev Salomon			change tires	
11:00	Ali Hasan		talk to Dr. Kim	Elma Jerena	
12:00	lunch	lunch	lunch	lunch	end of day
1:00	Alma Reynolds			Sue Lie	
2:00		Yuki Yamada		Stan Williams	
3:00	meeting cancelled				
4:00	pick up children		pick up children	Pedro Santos	pick up children
5:00					

Cultural Note   If you need to cancel an appointment, try to cancel it 24 hours in advance. Some doctors and dentists charge a fee if you don't cancel the appointment with enough notice.

REVIEW: GRAMMAR

Modals

This semester, you have learned about a very frequent type of verb in conversational English. This type of verb is called a *modal.* You have learned the modals *can, could, may, might, will,* and *would.* These verbs are very important because they can be used for a variety of purposes.

Modals (continued)

Modals can be used in many different ways.

To Ask Polite Questions:

- **Can** I have your name, please?
- **May** I see your ID?
- **Could** you show me your ID?

To Make Polite Requests:

- **Can** I use your cell phone?

To Express Doubt and Possibility:

- It **could** be an airplane.
- It **might** be Laura.

To Offer Help:

- You **could** talk to the nurse on campus.
- You **can** study with a tutor.
- You **may** want to meet with the teacher.

To Explain Problems/Express Inability:

- I **can't** go to work because I'm sick.

To Order in Restaurants:

- **I'll** have the salmon salad.
- **I'd** like a soda.

To Make an Invitation:

- **Would** you like to go shopping on the weekend?

Modal Rule 1: Affirmative Sentences

Modal verbs in affirmative sentences are always used between the subject and the verb.

For example:

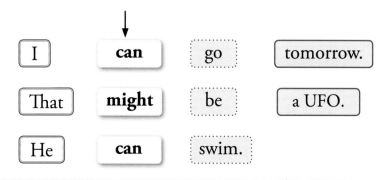

ACTIVITY **H** Write one sentence in the affirmative using a different modal for each purpose below.

Asking a polite question: _____

Making an invitation: _____

Offering help: _____

Modal Rule 2: Modals and Verbs

Modal verbs *never* change form and are always followed by the base form of the verb.

For example:

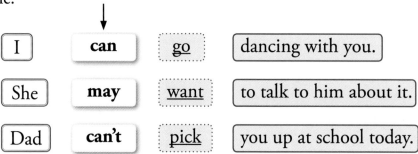

ACTIVITY **I**   With a partner, discuss the mistakes in the sentences below. Explain why each one is a mistake.

    a. He can dances very well.

    b. That may is a dog.

    c. They can't went.

    d. Could you to study with me?

GRAMMAR

Modal Rule 3: Negative Statements

The negative is always formed by adding *not* after the modal.

| I | can | + | not | go | tomorrow. |

Or, you can contract the negative.

| I | can't | go | tomorrow. |

ACTIVITY **J**   Put each set of words below in the correct order to make a sentence. Make sure you insert *not* in the right place. You can also contract *not* in your sentences.

| come | I | to school tomorrow | not | can |

a. _____

| may | you | not | go |

b. _____

| that | not | be | can | an airplane |

c. _____

| not | the bird | can | fly |

d. _____

Modal Rule 4: Questions with Modals

Questions are formed by putting the modal before the subject.

For example:

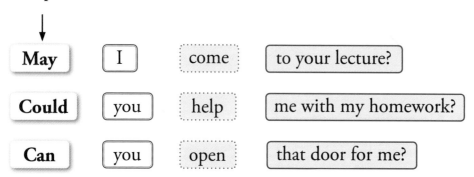

May	I	come	to your lecture?
Could	you	help	me with my homework?
Can	you	open	that door for me?

ACTIVITY **K** Read the situations below and write questions using modals.

a. You want to ask a friend to lend you five dollars.

_____

b. You want to invite a classmate to have lunch with you after class.

_____

c. You want to ask your teacher if you can leave early.

_____

d. You want to ask your neighbor if she can turn down the stereo.

_____

Modal Rule 5: Modals for Different Purposes

The same modal can be used for different purposes. For example:

Favor ⟶ **Can** I use your pen?

Impossibility ⟶ I **can't** go to school tomorrow because I have a doctor's appointment.

Suggestion ⟶ You **can** drink some tea before bed.

ACTIVITY **L**   Read the sentences below. Put the number that corresponds to the purpose of the modal used in each set of parentheses. More than one answer is possible for some items.

a. ( ) **May** I see your ID, please?

b. ( ) **Could** you help me with my homework?

c. ( ) **Would** you like to see a movie with me on Friday?

d. I think it ( ) **may** be a pen, or it ( ) **could** be a pencil.

e. I ( ) **can't** come tomorrow because I need to go to Los Angeles.

f. ( ) **I'll** have chicken alfredo, please.

g. You ( ) **could** try to study during your break, don't you think?

h. ( ) **Can** you open the door for me, please?

Purposes
1. Asking Questions Politely
2. Making Polite Requests
3. Expressing Doubt and Possibility
4. Offering Help
5. Talking about Problems/ Inability
6. Ordering in Restaurants
7. Inviting

ACTIVITY **M**   Work in groups of four. Choose one student to be the secretary. (The secretary is the only one who can record your group's answers.) Your teacher will choose one of the scenarios below. You will have one minute to write as many sentences with modals as you can. Do the same tasks for all the scenarios your teacher chooses to use.

Scenario 1: You are asking your neighbor for a big favor.

Scenario 2: You are inviting a close friend to do something or attend an event with you.

Scenario 3: You need to ask your teacher for permission to do something.

Scenario 4: You have to ask your mother/father/brother/sister a favor.

REVIEW: GRAMMAR

Connecting Thoughts with *So, And Then, And*, and *'Cause*

You can use *so, and then, and,* and *'cause* to connect your thoughts when you speak. It is important to remember these simple rules about these words. *First,* the most frequent connectors in spoken English are not the same as in written English. *Second,* you can repeat these connectors many times when speaking, but you cannot do that in writing.

ACTIVITY **N** Decide if each connector below is being used in speaking or in writing. Circle the correct answer. Then discuss with the class what things you used to make your decision.

a. I went to the grocery store . . . **and then** I returned the movies . . . **and** I also got to deposit the checks.

　　　　　　　Speaking　　　　　Writing

b. I went to the grocery store, **and then** I returned the movies. After that, I also deposited the checks.

　　　　　　　Speaking　　　　　Writing

c. I couldn't come yesterday **because** I had a flat tire on the way to school. It took me two hours to get it fixed, which caused me to get to school too late.

　　　　　　　Speaking　　　　　Writing

d. I couldn't come yesterday **'cause** I had a flat tire on the way to school . . . **and** it took me two hours to get it fixed . . . **so** I didn't get to school on time.

　　　　　　　Speaking　　　　　Writing

ACTIVITY **O** Complete each sentence with *so, and then, and,* or *'cause.*

A: What's up?

B: Hi. I'm having a pretty bad day today.

A: Oh?

B: Yeah, first I . . . I couldn't take a shower when I woke up . . .

A: Oh, no.

B: _____ there was no water in the building . . .
　　　　　(a)

A: That's terrible!

B: I know! _____ my car broke down on the way here.
　　　　　　　　(b)

A: Gee!

B: _____ I had to get it towed.
　　　(c)

A: Is the problem serious?

B: I don't know yet. They gave me a rental . . . anyway . . . _____
　　　　　　　　　　　　　　　　　　　　　　　　　　　(d)

　　I didn't get here when I needed to, _____ I missed my class.
　　　　　　　　　　　　　　　　　　　(e)

A: Just a class, though.

B: I know, but it was an important one.

A: I see.

Read the favors and invitations on the left. Then write an explanation for refusing each invitation or favor. In your explanation, connect three or more thoughts with one or more connectors.

Would you like to see a movie with me after class?	→	*Sorry. Carla invited me to go shopping with her **and then** have dinner, **so** I can't after class. Maybe some other time.*

Can I borrow ten dollars?	→	_____ _____

May I use your cell phone for just a second?	→	_____ _____

Would you like to get some coffee?	→	_____ _____

Could you help me study for the test tomorrow night?	→	_____ _____

Can you give me a ride home today?	→	_____ _____

Would you like to come over for lunch on Saturday?	→	_____ _____

ACTIVITY **Q** Half of the class will be Group A. The other half will be Group B. Students in Group A will prepare a favor to ask a neighbor. Students in Group B will have to refuse the favor using at least one connector. Stand up and move around the classroom. Practice with four classmates.

Being More Formal or Less Formal

When you speak, you can use more formal or less formal language depending on the situation. You can use modals to make your conversation more polite. For example:

> **Less Formal:** Your ID, please?
> **More Formal:** May I see your ID, please?

ACTIVITY **R** Read the interactions below. Circle + for more formal or − for less formal. Write where the conversation takes place and who is talking. Discuss your answers with the class.

CONVERSATION 1 (+ / −)

Where: _____

Who: _____

A: Yes, officer?

B: Your ID, please?

A: All right . . . here.

B: Uh-huh. Your proof of insurance?

A: Here.

B: OK.

A: What did I do wrong?

B: You didn't come to a complete stop.

A: I see.

B: I will give you a warning this time.

A: Thanks.

B: You need to be more careful.

A: I will. Thanks.

CONVERSATION 2 (+ / −)

Where: _____

Who: _____

A: Good morning. How may I help you?

B: I have a test scheduled for 10:00.

A: Oh, I see. . . . May I have your name, please?

B: Sure. It's Adriana Wright.

A: Oh, I see you have a 10:00 test in our counseling center. Could I see your ID, please?

B: Sure. . . . Here it is.

A: Thanks. You are all set, Ms. Wright.

B: Thanks.

A: Go to the first door on your right and someone will be there to help you.

B: Thanks a lot.

A: No problem.

ACTIVITY **S** Work in pairs. Each pair should choose one of the eight scenarios below. Create a short dialog and present it to the class. The other students have to guess who and where you are and if the interaction is formal or informal.

	Location	Formality
1. two classmates	cafeteria	informal
2. a teacher and a student	teacher's office	formal
3. two neighbors who don't know each other well	in front of a house	formal
4. two neighbors who know each other well	in front of a house	informal
5. two coworkers	in a meeting at work	formal
6. a customer and a salesperson	at a department store	formal
7. a customer and a salesperson	at a farmer's market	informal
8. your own idea _____	your own idea _____	your own idea _____

Reductions and Contractions

CD 3 Track 38

This semester, you have learned that when people speak English, they do not always pronounce all of the syllables. The most important words are *stressed* (pronounced longer and louder). Other words are *reduced* (two words pronounced as one) or *contracted* (two words combined by an apostrophe). Learning *reductions* and *contractions* helps you understand others better. Let's review some of the reductions and contractions you have learned.

Examples of Reductions	Examples of Contractions
I wanna = I want to	**I'm** = I am
I gotta = I've got to	**he's** = he is
I hafta = I have to	**isn't** = is not
I'm gonna = I'm going to	**I'd like** = I would like
	can't = cannot

◀)) ACTIVITY **T** Listen to the conversations. What reductions do you hear?
CD 3 Track 39

Conversation 1: _____

Conversation 2: _____

◀)) ACTIVITY **U** Listen to the conversations again. Write down the contractions you hear.
CD 3 Track 40

Conversation 1: _____

Conversation 2: _____

REVIEW AND EXPAND

ACTIVITY **A**   **1.** In groups of three or four, discuss the following questions:

    a. What couldn't you do at the beginning of the semester that you can do now?

    b. What have you learned that you had no idea about before?

    c. What do you think you need to work on?

Remember to...
- use modals when necessary.
- use the present, past, and future tenses.
- use connectors (*so, and, and then, 'cause*).
- use speaking strategies (hesitation, reaction, etc).
- use reductions and contractions.

2. Share your answers to the questions above with the rest of the class. Raise your hand when you want to speak.

ACTIVITY **B**   Work in groups of four and play the game on the next two pages. Each group needs a pair of dice. Each student will need a different coin to use as a marker. Place the coins on **START**. Decide who goes first, second, third, and fourth. Student 1 rolls the dice and moves his or her coin. Student 1 reads the instructions and does what is asked. The other students take turns doing the same. The first student to reach the finish line wins the game.

Remember to...
- hesitate.
- react to what your classmates say.
- ask for repetition and check understanding.
- talk around a word when you can't remember it or ask "How do you say . . .?"
- connect your thoughts with *so, then, and,* and *'cause.*
- be more or less polite depending on the situation.
- say "no" politely.

REVIEW AND EXPAND

	Talk about yourself for 1 minute.	Tell the other students about a bad/good/ strange dream you've had.	Invite someone in your group to do something. If he or she says no, insist.
START →			
Discuss your favorite foods. Find out the favorite foods of the other members of your group.	**GO BACK 4 SPACES**	Describe a classmate and let the other classmates guess who you are describing.	**LOSE A TURN** ←
What do you think we could do to protect our environment? Discuss your ideas. →	Talk about what you are going to do for vacation.	Tell what you have to do on the weekends.	Tell your classmates about a recipe you like.
GO BACK 2 SPACES	Discuss what you do to be healthy. Talk about any habits you could change to be healthier.	Tell what you did last weekend.	**SKIP 3 SPACES** ←
Ask to borrow something from one of your classmates. →	Tell what would you like to do in the future.	Try to find out as much as possible about your classmates' last weekend.	**ROLL THE DICE AGAIN**

(continued on the next page)

START: Tell what your favorite place to shop is. Ask your classmates if any of them like to shop at the same place. →	Ask your classmates a question. Use the future tense.	Talk about a problem and ask for a suggestion.	Talk about your plans for next semester.
GO AHEAD 1 SPACE 👎	Give your opinion about the book(s) your class used this semester.	**LOSE A TURN**	Think of different things you could do with a sheet of paper. ←
Discuss some things you think you need to do to speak even better English. →	**GO AHEAD 1 SPACE** 👉	Ask for a favor.	Give your opinion of all the classes you took this semester.
Invite your classmates to do something with you.	Tell about what computer skills you learned this semester that can help you improve your English.	**ROLL THE DICE AGAIN** 🎲	Ask your classmates a **BIG** favor. They have to give a good excuse. ←
Discuss why you are studying English.	Imagine an object and draw it. Have your classmates guess what it could be. →	Tell what country you would like to visit. Discuss why.	FINISH 🏃

EVALUATION

ACTIVITY **A** Now that you have completed the activities in this chapter, complete the self-evaluation checklist below. Discuss your checklist with a classmate.

Self-Evaluation Checklist

- ☐ I was able to make an appointment.
- ☐ I began and ended interactions politely.
- ☐ I used modals.
- ☐ I made invitations with *would* or *want*.
- ☐ I asked for a favor politely.

I used the following structures (Circle all that apply):

Past   Present   Future   Inability   Desire   Obligation

- ☐ I started and ended interactions appropriately.
- ☐ I said "no" politely.
- ☐ I gave an excuse when I said "no."
- ☐ I connected my thoughts with *so, and then, and*, and *'cause*.
- ☐ I asked for repetition, spelling, and clarification when necessary.
- ☐ I checked and confirmed information when necessary.
- ☐ I was able to be more or less formal, depending on the situation.

ACTIVITY **B** Look back at the chapter and the self-evaluation checklist above. What can you do this week to improve the skills you have learned in this chapter? Talk with a partner and write an action plan for how you can improve your skills this week.

Example When I use modals, I sometimes use *to* after them. I need to remember not to do that. So, I have decided to focus on that every time I use modals in my speech and writing. I also need to use a larger variety of modals. I usually use only *can*.

Action Plan

CHAPTER 3

REVIEW AND EXPAND

ACTIVITY C   PAGE 45

1. Work in groups of four. Use the cards below or make 10 cards with the name of an object on each card. Trade cards with another group.

2. Place the cards face down in a pile. The first student takes a card and talks around the object by describing the object as if he or she didn't know the name of it. The other three students guess what the object is. The first student to guess correctly keeps the card. The goal of the game is to collect as many cards as possible.

CAT	SUNGLASSES	PHOTO	DOOR	PEN
BOOK	SOFA	HAIRBRUSH	UMBRELLA	CAR
CUP	CAMERA	SHAMPOO	HAT	COAT
DOG	SHOES	SPOON	COMPUTER	BICYCLE

Heinle, Cengage Learning © 2010 Photocopiable

CHAPTER 4

REVIEW AND EXPAND

ACTIVITY **A** PAGES 62-63

As a class, role-play a scene at a formal restaurant. One student plays the restaurant host or hostess. This person greets and seats each party. The rest of the class divides into groups of three—two people act as customers and the third person acts as their server. After the host or hostess has seated everyone, he or she can join the last party as a customer or as the server.

Use the steps for what happens at a restaurant on page 63 as a guide for your role play.

Use the menu below to order.

Menu

Appetizers	*Entrées*	*Desserts*	*Drinks*
Spinach Dip	Grilled Salmon	Fruit Tart	Iced Tea
Potato Skins	Sesame Chicken	Blueberry Pie	Coffee
Garlic Bread	Pasta Primavera	Apple Pastry	Soda
	(vegetarian)	Fudge Cake	Sparkling Water
	Barbecued Steak		

Every entrée comes with a choice of a small salad, rice or potatoes (mashed or baked), and a vegetable (squash, corn, or peas).

Heinle, Cengage Learning © 2010 Photocopiable

CHAPTER 6

LEARN AND PRACTICE

ACTIVITY S PAGE 97

1. Work in groups of four. Use the problem cards below and solution cards on the next page.

2. Place the problem cards face down in a pile.

3. Divide the solution cards between your group members. Each student displays the solution cards on the desk so everybody can see them.

4. The first student starts by picking a problem card. This student has to explain his or her problem to the group.

5. The other group members check their solution cards. If you think one of the solutions fits the problem, make a suggestion using *then*.

6. If the solution makes sense, the student with the problem accepts the suggestion by saying, "That's a great idea. Thanks." If it does not make sense, or if it is not a good suggestion, the student politely rejects the suggestion and gives a brief explanation by saying, "I'm sorry. I don't think that'll work."

7. Take turns picking up a problem card until all the problem cards have been used.

Problem Cards

Problem: I have to write a difficult paper.	**Problem:** My best friend is angry with me.	**Problem:** My computer is not working. I don't have the money for a new one.	**Problem:** My cat is sick, and I don't have the money for a veterinarian.

Problem: I travel next week to see my family, but I can't afford my train ticket.	**Problem:** I need to do a lot of laundry, but I don't have a washer/dryer at home.	**Problem:** My rent is too high.	**Problem:** I need to organize my office, but I don't know how to start.

Heinle, Cengage Learning © 2010 Photocopiable

Solution Cards

Suggestion: Get a tutor.	**Suggestion:** Get a loan.	**Suggestion:** Send him or her a letter.	**Suggestion:** Use the Laundromat.

Suggestion: Use a credit card.	**Suggestion:** Hire a professional.	**Suggestion:** Get a roommate.	**Suggestion:** Sell an item.

Heinle, Cengage Learning © 2010 Photocopiable

LEARN AND PRACTICE

ACTIVITY **F**   PAGE 108

1. In groups of three or four, play a concentration game with irregular verbs. Each group should make 16 cards. Or use the cards below. Eight cards should have the base form of an irregular verb. The other eight cards should have the simple past tense of each base form. Trade cards with another group.

2. Place the cards face down in a square with four cards going across and four cards going down. The first student should flip over two cards. If the two cards are the base form and the simple past tense form of the same verb, it is a match. If the cards don't make a match, the student should turn the cards back over. The other students each take turns trying to make a match. When a student makes a match, he or she keeps the cards. The goal of the game is to try to collect as many cards as possible.

GOT	MADE	TELL	WROTE
TOLD	HAVE	HAD	GAVE
SEE	GET	GIVE	MAKE
TAKE	WRITE	SAW	TOOK

Heinle, Cengage Learning © 2010 Photocopiable

REVIEW AND EXPAND

ACTIVITY B   PAGE 120

Your instructor will give each student a card. Get up and talk to six different people. Greet them and ask about the weekend. Remember to react to the answers and make comments.

Card 1:

TERRIBLE!
What/where: went to the beach
When: on Saturday
What happened: birds ate our food when we were in the water

Card 2:

AWESOME!
What/where: went out to eat
When: Sunday afternoon
What happened: didn't have to pay

Card 3:

BORING!
What: stayed home and cleaned the house
When: Saturday
What happened: nothing

Card 4:

GREAT!
What: went to a fondue party
When: Saturday night
What happened: Lots of people were there; everybody danced and told stories

Heinle, Cengage Learning © 2010 Photocopiable